DRAMATIZED BALLADS

THE PRETTY DRUMMER

DRAMATIZED BALLADS

by

ALICE M. G. WHITE
· and ·
JANET E. TOBITT

ILLUSTRATIONS by
BARBARA DANIELSEN

E. P. DUTTON & CO. INC.
NEW YORK

First Printing — April 1937
Second Printing — September 1938
Third Printing — May 1943
Fourth Printing — April 1946
Fifth Printing — December 1950
Sixth Printing — January 1955

INTRODUCTION

THE delightful possibilities of the folk ballad for dramatization are gradually being realized. Many people, in the unfruitful search for children's plays which have real dramatic interest, and human values, are discovering in folk poetry a solution to their problem.

In this book we offer suggestions for the presentation of ballads* in dramatic form, with the hope that they may be of service. Our ideas have developed gradually, from experimentation in ballad play-making with children, and with adults, who, incidentally, enjoy participating in this kind of entertainment, which may be as simple as a game, or as sophisticated as a Chauve Souris production.

Folk balladry contains dramatic possibilities, since like all folk material it is essentially human. The brothers Grimm once said that they had never found a lie in folklore. Though ballads frequently have fantastic plots they are founded upon a shrewd observation of life, and their understanding of human motives is often penetrating.

The very fact that this wealth of folk literature has prevailed throughout the centuries is good argument in its favor. Also, we are by no means innovators when we put ballads on the stage. Hundreds of years ago our ancestors recognized their possibilities. In the Middle Ages songs were frequently accompanied by pantomime while in Elizabethan times acted ballads were presented on the popular stages at the close of the full-length plays. In his book, *The Elizabethan Jig* † Mr. Charles Read Baskervill throws light upon these ballad dramatizations, many of which he reproduces with detailed contemporary stage directions. He cites "The Barrin' of the Door" as a popular "play" in Shakespeare's time; today it still

---

* We use the term "ballad" to denote a folk song which tells a story and has dramatic possibilities.
† *The Elizabethan Jig and Related Song Drama*, Charles Read Baskervill (University of Chicago Press, Chicago, Ill., 1929).

5

causes delight by its homely wit. There is nothing new under the sun. Generations have put the old ballads to the test, finding them real in content, satisfying to the mind and heart—a good recommendation, surely.

Then, the plot of the ballad is usually simple and forthright. It is almost entirely objective, often breathtakingly swift in its development. Fair maidens are wooed and won, shrews are converted into dutiful wives in the twinkling of an eye. All is accomplished with a magnificent disregard for useless preliminaries. The actors have no time to lose no chance to settle gradually into their parts. It is 'do or die' from the start—a challenge which the young players are eager to accept. Also the children are spared the tedium of learning parts. They must, of course, know the details of the ballad, and in some instances memorize a few lines. Their task, however, is comparatively simple, and rehearsals need not occupy a disproportionate amount of time. Moreover each child has a chance to assume many rôles.

Characterization in the ballad is correspondingly direct and clearly defined. Here are no introverts, no problems for the psychoanalyst, but normal specimens of humanity. We are shown the lover, the mercenary pappa, the jealous sister, the flirt, the hen-pecked husband,—to mention a few typical examples. The lover exerts all the charms at his command, the hen-pecked husband defies his spouse at the inevitable moment—so with all these ballad people. They run true to form and are easily characterized.

A distinctive feature of the ballad is the pulsing regularity of its rhythm. The swing of the verse demands rhythmic delivery of the poetry, rhythmic movement, rhythmic gesture. Most children are quick to sense the lilt of the poetry, eager to reproduce it in their own voices and bodily movements. Even the less musical ones are soon carried along by the easy swing of the verse, the feeling for

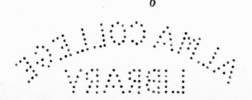

which may be accentuated by having the players walk round the room to the beat of the rhythm, as a preliminary exercise.

MUSIC IN FOLK SONG AND BALLADRY

How to sing the ballads. The lyrical quality of the ballad is manifested in its music and as far as possible in this book we have chosen examples having their own traditional tunes. In singing these we are carrying on the art of the minstrels of old who sang their wondrous tales to enthralled listeners. There is no point in singing unless the story is made clear, therefore, particular regard must be paid to precise enunciation and to correct expression on the part of the singers. The rhythm too, must be kept in full swing so that music, words, and action, present one harmonious pattern. Good articulation on the part of a few singers, or even a soloist, leads to better tone quality than indifferent singing by many, though in the case of a well-known or easily-learnt song, pleasing variety may occasionally be obtained by inviting the audience to join in, and so feel part of the "show". However, in the main, we have found that a chorus of from four to twelve voices is sufficient for general purposes; they should be well rehearsed in the lights and shades of the song. It breaks the monotony, especially in the case of a long ballad, if "dialogue" lines are sung by individual singers possessing good carrying voices. Failing these, the group may be divided to take the singing parts of the "characters", the whole chorus singing the narrative or refrain in ensemble.

Instrumental Music. Unaccompanied singing in balladry is the oldest and perhaps the most natural form; reliance of the singers on a piano, with elaborate accompaniment, or pseudo-"descriptive" improvisations, finds no part in real folk-singing, which is spontaneous, impersonal, and independent of harmonic support. Where incidental music is required the most pleasing effects may be obtained by the use of a fiddle, shepherd's pipe, or similarly unsophisticated instrument; where there is no traditional air be sure to use what is essentially in keeping for incidental music. For instance, one would not use an English dance tune in the production of a French ballad.

Nature of Ballad Music. "Evolved," or Folk Music, expresses universal truths in few notes, but often possesses rare melodic beauty, on account of which it has survived the test of time; imagination had to be compressed into the limited scope of sixteen bars or so, which by sheer attractiveness give proof of their stability in their urge to repetition. Simplicity and directness of statement in the words find their counterpart in the music, nor were the traditional singers upset by varying lengths of the lines of different verses. Choirs accompanying acted ballads must practise carefully the fitting in of extra syllables to ensure clear utterance, but in the main the singing difficulties are few. Folk music is as wide and as deep as the understanding of its interpreters, it runs the gamut of human emotion, and is universal in its appeal to every manner and mood. A tangible realization of the "dramatic" quality of old ballads brings to children especially a deeper appreciation of their music.

CHOICE OF MATERIAL

Every ballad or folk song, however, is not suitable for dramatization, and failure to achieve satisfactory results is often due to a poor choice of material. The importance of selecting ballads containing dramatic action cannot be over-estimated, for drama *is* action. Old songs and ballads, which are reflective rather than active, prove uninteresting when given pictorial form. Choose ballads in which changes of mood occur, in which "something happens". The audience enjoys being held in suspense and is likely to become restive if the action being witnessed turns out to be slight and uneventful. Plenty of stimulating material does exist, however, from which dramatic "hits" can be fashioned. Before selecting a ballad for dramatic interpretation ask yourself these questions: Does it contain an element of suspense? Has it variety of tempo? Does the action work up to a climax? If your ballad stands these tests it is undoubtedly

INTRODUCTION

an interesting one with which to experiment; it will be popular with the players, and "good theatre" at the same time. Apart from the ballads and songs actually worked out in this book there is a supplementary list of suitable material, with sources.

It will be found in the examples worked out and in the list of recommended ballads that they may be grouped roughly under several headings. Many are of the "wooing" type, such as "Where are you going to, my pretty maid?" or "Oh, no John". Others, such as "The Barrin' of the Door", "The Old Man Can't Keep His Wife at Home", and "The Dumb Wife Cured" caricature domestic strife. A large number deal with pure romance, often between people of different stations in life, for instance, "The Bailiff's Daughter of Islington" and "Green Broom". Many, such as "The Bold Pedlar and Robin Hood" depict physical combat. Some ballads include several of the elements mentioned above. "Sir Eglamore" may be considered pure farce, and "Auld Robin Gray" is a simple tragedy.

Ballads may be acted by groups of almost any size. "Dashing Away with a Smoothing Iron" requires only one player, while "The Uninvited Aunt" or "Rataplan" may contain innumerable characters.

Many are equally suitable for presentation indoors or out-of-doors. A number of them, such as the Robin Hood ones, or "The Green Wedding", are particularly effective in a woodland setting.

METHODS OF DRAMATIZATION

Just as in folk-dancing, the precision of movement and the perfect rhythmic interpretation of the spirit of the ballad should be maintained. The group, after choosing typical gestures and movements suitable to the action in the ballad, should decide to follow definitely the pattern agreed upon. Exaggeration of movement is recommended. Throughout the whole production the rhythm of the ballad must continue inevitably, like the ticking of a clock.

INTRODUCTION

Great variety is possible in the linking of the narrative and the action. A program of ballads need never suffer from monotony of presentation.

(a) A soloist may sing the ballad as it is pantomimed silently by the actors. A chorus may sing the refrain, if any occurs.

(b) A soloist or a chorus may sing the narrative part of the ballad, and the actors sing the dialogue.

(c) A chorus may sing the entire ballad being pantomimed by the players. On occasion the chorus may dress in costume, stand on the stage, and reflect the mood of the action.

(d) A reader may narrate the story and the actors speak any dialogue which occurs. Incidental traditional music may be interspersed between the verses.

(e) Folk dancing may frequently be introduced, particularly in a ballad which is gay and has a long chorus. ("Ballad" and "ballet" are from similar origins and early songs were often danced, and dances were frequently sung.) By the same token, when the action seems too swift, and the chorus is short or non-existent, music may be introduced between the verses, while the characters dance, or in some other way express the mood of the preceding stanza. A musical introduction and conclusion often help to make the beginning and end of the play smooth and more delightful.

(f) Sometimes when only two characters are required to portray the action, four or even six, may be introduced, so that two or three sets of players are interpreting the theme. Interesting groupings and variety can thus be achieved for the audience. A definite pattern must be worked out to secure balance, prevent confusion, and maintain the rhythm.

INTRODUCTION

(g) In the case of "ballad poems," or songs which have music difficult or unattractive in rendition, a reader may narrate the story on one side of the stage, while the actors interpret the events in silent pantomime, or

(h) A group of readers may recite the ballad in unison, while the players interpret the action. A verse-speaking choir can be as effective as a singing chorus.

The various methods for ballads with music are demonstrated in the examples chosen in this book. The details of presentation, however, are not meant to be arbitrary; they are merely offered as practical suggestions. Children enjoy creating the action for themselves and show great imagination in interpretation. From the supplementary list a wealth of material may be gathered and original patterns worked out. Such variety is possible that one may divide the acting group into several parts, letting each create its own interpretation, the results being compared for dramatic effectiveness. The educational benefits from such a project are obvious.

The terms L. and R. refer to the actors' Left and Right as they face the audience; "upstage" means the part of the stage farthest from the audience, "downstage" that which is nearest.

SETTINGS AND PROPERTIES

The ballad-play is not extravagant in its demands for incidentals. The setting may be a corner of a classroom, an unpretentious platform in a club-room, or a stage rejoicing in elaborate backdrops and handsome velvet curtains. Where facilities are meagre the imagination supplies the realism which limited equipment withholds. Properties more difficult to come by than chairs, benches, and tables, can easily be dispensed with, in which case even greater sincerity has to be infused into the pantomime by the actors, who gain rather than lose by the lack of material aids. Where a property heightens the effect of realism and does not impede the action, it may be used at the discretion of the group.

Costuming may be simple or elaborate, according to the facilities available. The main point is that it should be effective and in keeping with the "atmosphere" of the play. Care should be taken to see that the dresses are fresh-looking and well-pressed; they must be worn carefully, with an eye to "line" and the whole effect should be artistic and colorful. We append a short bibliography of reference books for stage costuming.

Elaborate make-up is unnecessary, and may be dispensed with altogether in simple presentations. Even in more pretentious productions a grease-paint foundation need not be used, dry rouge and powder being entirely adequate.

For young characters cheek rouge is applied high on the cheekbones, while wrinkles for old characters are put on with a maroon-colored liner, not with black. In a stage production the eyes should be accentuated by eye shadow, and outlined with a black or blue liner.

Crêpe-hair supplies beards and moustaches, the latter being applied in two parts on the upper lip, with a slight space between them. Sparing use of crêpe-hair in the construction of beards produces the best results; care must be taken, however, to stick it beneath the chin and jaws. Generous application of spirit-gum as a foundation is a safeguard against the loss of a cherished whisker during the performance.

INTRODUCTION

BIBLIOGRAPHY

For research   The English and Scottish Popular Ballads, by Professor Child. (Houghton, Mifflin and Co.)

For piping   Shepherds' Pipes, How to Make and Play Them, by Janet E. Tobbit. (Girl Scouts, Inc.)

For costuming   A History of Everyday Things in England, Vol. 1, by Marjorie and C. H. B. Quennell. (B. T. Batsford)

The Bankside Costume Book, by Melicent Stone, (Wells Gardner, Darton). Instructions given here for making mediaeval dresses.

Shakespeare for Community Players, by Roy Mitchell, (Dent). (Advice on staging and costuming Shakespearian plays applies to ballad-plays)

Costuming a Play, by Elizabeth Grimball and Rhea Wells. (Century Co.)

The Story of Costume told in Pictures, by Belle Northrup. (Art Education Press, Inc., 424 Madison Avenue, New York City)

American and other costumes are described in books by Frances Haire. (A. S. Barnes and Co.)

CONTENTS

I. *AULD ROBIN GRAY*

I. AULD ROBIN GRAY

Scottish
Lady Anne Lindsay

Slowly, with much expression

1- Young Jam-ie lo'd me weel, and sought me for his bride, But

sav - ing a crown, he had nae-thing else be - side; To

make the crown a pound, my Jam - ie gaed to sea, And the

crown and the pound were baith for me. He

had - na been gane a week but on - ly twa, When my

fa - ther brake his arm and our cow was stown a way; My

mi - ther she fell sick, my Jam - ie at the sea, And

auld Rob - in Gray cam a - court - - - - - ing me.

I. AULD ROBIN GRAY

2. My father couldna work—my mither couldna spin;
   I toil'd day and night, but their bread I couldna win;
   Auld Rob maintain'd them baith, and, wi' tears in his e'e,
   Said, "Jenny, for their sakes, will you marry me?"
   My heart it said "na," I look'd for Jamie back;
   But the wind it blew high, and the ship it was a wrack;
   The ship it was a wrack! Why didna Jenny dee?
   Oh why was I spar'd to cry, "Wae's me!"

3. My father urged me sair — my mither didna speak
   But she look'd in my face til my heart was like to break;
   So I gi'ed him my hand, tho' my heart was at the sea;
   And auld Robin Gray is gudeman to me.
   I hadna been a wife, a week but only four,
   When sittin' sae mournfully at my ain door,
   I saw my Jamie's wraith — I couldna think it he,
   Till he said, "I'm come hame, my love, to marry thee!"

4. O sair did we greet, and mickle did we say;
   We took but ae kiss, and we tore ourselves away.
   I wish that I were dead, but I'm no like to dee;
   Oh why do I live to say, "O wae's me!"
   I gang like a ghaist, and I carena to spin;
   I darena think o' Jamie, for that wad be a sin;
   But I'll do my best a gude wife aye to be,
   For auld Robin Gray is a kind man to me.

I. AULD ROBIN GRAY

PRESENTATION: The unusual feature of this ballad is its monologue form. As it would obviously be unrealistic dramatically to have Jenny sing throughout the entire action, a soloist offstage should be responsible for the song, while the players silently interpret the events to the audience.

STAGING: The scene is the interior of a poor farmer's cottage in Scotland. At the back centre is the entrance, and to the right of it a chair; also on the right, farther downstage, are a stool and a spinning-wheel. On stage left is a fireplace, on the upstage side of which stands a bench; on the opposite side of the fireplace, downstage, is a chair or stool. Downstage right is a door leading to another part of the farm. These are the essential details, others however may be added if a greater effect of realism is desired.

COSTUMING: Jenny should wear a plaid skirt and neat white bodice; her mother's skirt is drab, and the older woman wears a shawl over her head and shoulders; the father should have shabby trousers, worn shirt and waistcoat, with perhaps a handkerchief knotted round his neck. Robin, in contrast, sports a handsome outfit, including a warm muffler and a tam o' shanter. Jamie's clothes are neat but threadbare-looking; he may wear a kilt in verse 1, and change into seaman's trousers before his re-appearance in verse 3.

ACTION: The interpretation of a domestic tragedy in little is the responsibility of the actors who undertake this ballad. Sincerely acted, it has a most moving effect; certainly it contains the elements of which drama is made. As in "Rataplan" the musical accompaniment should be used only as a background for the action, rigid stylization detracting from the naturalness and the simplicity of this tragic story.

VERSE 1.

Young Jamie lo'd me weel, and sought me for his bride,

18

AULD ROBIN GRAY

Jamie enters R. with his arm round Jenny. They walk across the stage, gazing into each other's eyes, and sit on the bench by the fireplace.

But saving a crown, he had naething else beside;
Jamie looks at her longingly, but sadly, pulling out of his pocket his only crown.

To make the crown a pound, my Jamie went to sea,
He rises with determination, assisting Jenny to her feet and together they walk over to the door of the cottage.

And the crown and the pound were baith for me.
They kiss; Jamie bids Jenny farewell and departs.

REPEAT LINES 3–4 (the soloist singing with half-voice)

Jenny, by the door, sadly watches his departing figure, waving her hand, then returns slowly to the bench by the hearth where she sits gazing thoughtfully into the fire.

He hadna been gane a week but only twa,
She remains in this attitude. Her mother enters from R., goes to the spinning-wheel, sits down and begins to toil wearily.

When my father brake his arm & our cow was stown away;
The father enters R., his arm in a sling. Jenny rises and assists him to the bench, where he sits dejectedly. The mother continues to spin apathetically.

My mither she fell sick, my Jamie at the sea,
The mother collapses on her chair; Jenny goes over to her, comforts and revives her.

And auld Robin Gray cam a-courting me.
She continues to attend to her mother; the father remains in abject

AULD ROBIN GRAY

misery; Robin Gray appears in the doorway, removes his hat and takes in the situation.

VERSE 2. *My father couldna work — my mither couldna spin;*
I toil'd day and night, but their bread I couldna win;

Robin walks over to Jenny's side, helps her to raise her mother to her feet, and assists the old woman over to the chair by the fire. Jenny watches him with gratitude, sits at the spinning-wheel and works hopelessly.

Auld Rob maintained them baith, and, wi' tears in his e'e

The old couple sit as before; Robin gives the old man some money and then walks over to Jenny.

Said, "Jenny, for their sakes, will you marry me?"

Jenny rises, Robin puts his right arm about her, and places his left hand on his heart as he looks into her agitated face.

My heart it said "na," I look'd for Jamie back;
But the wind it blew high, and the ship it was a wrack;
The ship it was a wrack! Why didna Jenny dee?

The old man and wife are aghast when Jenny brushes past Robin and goes to the door. She stares out eagerly. The conflict going on in her mind must be made obvious by her facial expression. She occasionally turns her head to see what her father and mother are thinking, and to look with ill-concealed reluctance at Auld Robin, who stands watching her devotedly.

Oh why was I spar'd to cry, "Wae's me!"

She turns tragically from the doorway, and stands quite listlessly in the centre of the stage. The others do not move.

VERSE 3. *My father urged me sair — my mither didna speak*
But she look'd in my face till my heart was like to break;

The father goes over to Jenny, standing on her left, and appears to urge her into marriage with Robin, who stands, looking diffident, on her other side. Her mother remains in her chair, gazing at her with mute appeal.

So I gie'd him my hand, tho' my heart was at the sea;
Jenny gives him her hand hesitatingly, at the same time looking over her shoulder in the direction of the sea. The old couple show great pleasure; the mother rises.

And auld Robin Gray is gudeman to me.
The mother kisses her daughter, the father shakes hands with Robin.

REPEAT LINES 3–4 (the soloist singing with
half-voice)

The old couple exchange knowing glances, and depart R. Robin embraces Jenny, then they both go to the centre doorway, and he walks out happily, leaving her alone.

I hadna been a wife, a week, but only four,
When sittin' sae mournfully at my ain door,
Jenny sits down on the seat by the door, her hands in her lap, gazing listlessly out of doors and sighing.

I saw my Jamie's wraith — I couldna think it he,
She starts to her feet, and stands transfixed.

Till he said, "I'm come hame, my love, to marry thee!"
Jamie appears in the doorway and approaches her with arms outstretched.

VERSE 4. *O sair did we greet, and mickle did we say;*
  We took but ae kiss, and we tore ourselves away.
They embrace, then she shows him her wedding-ring. Looking heart-broken, he kisses her, and leaves her abruptly.

AULD ROBIN GRAY

I wish that I were dead, but I'm no like to dee;
Oh why do I live to say, "O wae's me!"
Jenny breaks down, crying piteously as she stands by the door through which Jamie has vanished.

I gang like a ghaist, and I carena to spin;
She wanders aimlessly over to the spinning-wheel, and gives it a half-hearted turn.

I darena think o' Jamie, for that wad be a sin;
Robin enters from R. and walks over to her.

But I'll do my best a gude wife aye to be,
She smiles at him wanly, fetches his pipe from the mantelshelf.

For auld Robin Gray is a kind man to me.
He accepts the pipe gratefully, putting his arm round her shoulders.

REPEAT LINES 7–8 (the soloist singing with
half-voice)

They walk out R., smiling at each other affectionately.

II. *THE BARRIN' OF THE DOOR*

II. THE BARRIN' OF THE DOOR

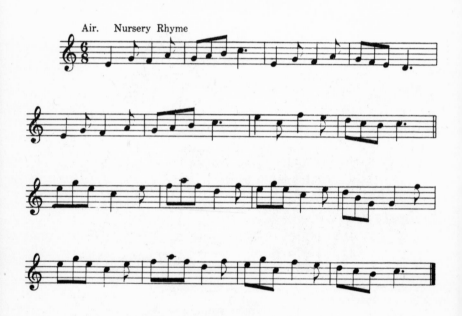

Air.   Nursery Rhyme

II. THE BARRIN' OF THE DOOR

1.

Narrator:

It fell aboot the Martinmas time,
And a gay time it was then,
When oor guid wife got puddin's to make,
And she boiled them in the pan.

2.

The wind sae cauld blew south and north
And blew into the floor;
Quoth our guid man to our guid wife,

Man:

"Gang oot and bar the door!"

3.

Wife:

"My hand is in my hussyfskap,
Guid man, as ye may see,
An it shouldna' be barr'd this hundred year,
It'll no' be barr'd by me."

4.

Narrator:

They made a paction 'twixt them twa,
They made it firm and sure,
That the first word whae'er should speak
Should rise and bar the door.

5.

Then by there came twa gentlemen
At twelve o'clock at nicht,
And they could neither see hoose nor hall,
Nor coal nor candle licht.

6.

First
gentleman:

"Now whether is this a rich man's hoose,
Or whether is it a poor?"

THE BARRIN' OF THE DOOR

Narrator: But ne'er a word wad ane o' them speak,
             For barrin' of the door.

7.

And first they ate the white puddin's
And then they ate the black.
Tho' muckle thocht the guid wife to hersel',
Yet ne'er a word she spak.

8.

First   "Here, man, tak' ye my knife;
gentleman: Then said the ane unto the ither —
             Do ye tak' off the auld man's beard,
             And I'll kiss the guid wife."

9.

Second   "But there's nae water in the hoose,
gentleman: And what shall we do than?"
First   "What ails ye at the puddin'-bree
gentleman: That's boilin' in the pan?"

10.

Narrator: O up then started oor guid man,
             An angry man was he:
Man: "Will ye kiss my wife before my een,
             And sca'd me wi' puddin'-bree?"

11.

Narrator: Then up and started oor guid wife,
             Gied three skips on the floor:
Wife: "Guid man, ye've spak the foremost word!
             Gang oot and bar the door!"

II. THE BARRIN' OF THE DOOR

PRESENTATION: This ballad is particularly effective when recited by a narrator (with Scottish accent, if possible!) while the action is pantomimed by the players, who may speak the lines of dialogue where they occur. Incidental music may be introduced to mark the rhythm and add humor to the scene. A fiddle or shepherd's pipe will do equally well.

STAGING: In the centre is a table (which may be covered by a plaid rug), with a chair on each side of it. A candle on the table is an effective touch. Downstage L. is a small table on which stand two large wooden bowls and two large cooking spoons.

COSTUMING: The good man should wear a tartan tam o' shanter and muffler, dark jacket and breeches. His beard, an important part of his make-up, should look as natural as possible. (To achieve a natural effect see instructions on make-up in the introduction.) If the performance is impromptu, attach a beard of cotton-batting to the ears so that it will come off easily at the crisis of the play. The good wife should wear a tartan shawl, a blouse, and a voluminous skirt. The robbers have large hats, cloaks and boots. The narrator is covered by a long cloak.

ACTION: As introductory bars are played (the whole of the incidental music once through), enter from R. the good man, who sits at the table; enter simultaneously from L. the good wife, who goes to the bowls and begins to stir them alternately with the spoons. The old man slaps himself to keep up his circulation, blows his knuckles, rubs his knees, in time with the music, while the wife stirs rhythmically. The lilt of the music should be animated and well accented. The narrator carries out the same rhythm in his reading of the verses.

VERSE I. The old man pantomimes extreme discomfort from cold; the wife stirs her puddings without looking up.

THE BARRIN' OF THE DOOR

Verse 2. They continue until line 4 when the old man says crossly, "Gang oot and bar the door," gesturing with his thumb towards the entrance. The wife regards him angrily.

Verse 3.

> *"My hand is in my hussfyskap,*
> *Guid man, as ye may see,*

The wife points to her bowl, takes a step or two towards the man.

> *An it shouldna be barr'd this hundred year,*
> *It'll no be barr'd by me."*

The wife wags her finger at her husband, indicating her disinclination to comply with his request. He looks angrily at her throughout the verse.

The incidental music is now played once through, while the wife starts walking indignantly round the table, followed by the husband, protesting and arguing with her. They keep step with the music. After circling the table twice, she plumps down in the chair R., he in the chair L., on the last note.

Verse 4.

> *They made a paction 'twixt them twa,*
> *They made it firm and sure,*

The couple face each other, beating the table with their fists four times to denote determination. (On "made", " 'twixt", "made", and "sure".)

> *That the first word wha'er should speak*

The man, using the right hand, wags his forefinger twice at his wife; she, using the left hand, wags her forefinger twice at him.

> *Should rise and bar the door.*

Using the same hands, each jerks a thumb in the direction of the

THE BARRIN' OF THE DOOR

door; they turn their backs towards each other on the last word of the verse.

VERSE 5.

Enter the first robber from L. the second robber from R. They prowl about the stage, taking large surreptitious strides in time with the beat of narration. They pantomime an examination of the room and its contents. They meet behind the centre table at the end of the verse. The man and wife show horror, but determination not to speak.

VERSE 6.

> "Now whether is this a rich man's hoose,
> Or whether is it a poor?"

The first robber asks the question of his companion, as they prowl about, peering rudely at the old couple.

> But ne'er a word wad ane o' them speak,
> For barrin' of the door.

They continue to explore. The couple sit terrified, but in stubborn silence.

The incidental music is played halfway through, during which the second robber takes four steps towards the pudding bowls and starts upon noticing their contents. He takes four steps back to his companion, excitedly, and urges the other along. They now both take four steps towards the bowls. They smack their lips, rubbing their stomachs in anticipation as the music ends.

VERSE 7.

> And first they ate the white puddin's
> And then they ate the black.
> Though muckle thocht the guid wife to hersel',

THE BARRIN' OF THE DOOR

The two robbers seize the spoons, dip deep into the bowls, extract large (imaginary) supplies of pudding, and eat, taking a mouthful on each line. The good man and his wife rise, drawing closer together. She clutches him for protection, peering over his shoulder; they lean forward as the robbers dip into the bowls and shrink back as the food disappears down their throats, all four characters bending down and back in unison and in time with the recitation.

> *Yet ne'er a word she spak.*

The good wife takes a few steps away from her husband; the good man sits down as the thieves finish their meal.

VERSE 8.

> *Then said the ane unto the ither —*

The robbers survey the old couple.

> *"Here, man, tak' ye my knife;*

The first robber offers the other his knife.

> *Do ye tak' off the old man's beard,*
> *And I'll kiss the guid wife."*

He pantomimes cutting off the beard and kissing the wife. The old man looks alarmed; the wife may look annoyed, or coy, according to her fancy!

VERSE 9.

> *"But there's nae water in the hoose,*
> *And what shall we do than?"*

The second robber indicates lack of water.

> *"What ails ye at the puddin'-bree*
> *That's boilin' in the pan?"*

The first robber points to the pudding bowl, and on the word "pan" rushes over to the wife to kiss her. The secoond robber cuts off the old man's beard.

THE BARRIN' OF THE DOOR

> *O up then started oor guid man,*
> *An angry man was he:*

The old man jumps up indignantly.

> *"Will ye kiss my wife before my een,*

He pushes the first robber, who drops to the ground.

> *And sca'd me wi' puddin'-bree?"*

The old man now pushes the second robber, who also falls. (The fight is not actual; the robbers must fall upon a touch, otherwise the action is muddled.)

VERSE 11.

> *Then up and started oor guid wife,*

The good wife preens herself.

> *Gied three skips on the floor:*

She gives three skips.

> *"Guid man, ye've spak the foremost word!*
> *Gang oot and bar the door!"*

Saying her speech triumphantly she signals to the door. The old man looks crestfallen.

The incidental music is played once through. The wife dances round the table, hand in hand with the robbers. Then the three dance off, L. or R. waving good-bye to the old man, who picks up his beard sadly and goes out the opposite way, shaking his head and looking dismally at his shorn whiskers.

III. *THE DARK EYED SAILOR*

111. THE DARK EYED SAILOR

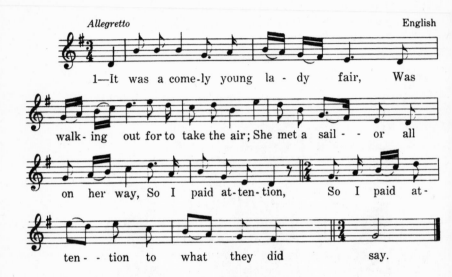

Allegretto

English

1—It was a come-ly young la - dy fair, Was walk-ing out for to take the air; She met a sail - - or all on her way, So I paid at-ten-tion, So I paid at-ten - - tion to what they did say.

III. THE DARK EYED SAILOR

2. Said William, "Lady, why walk alone?
   The night is coming and the day near gone."
   She said, while tears from her eyes did fall,
   "It's a dark eyed sailor,
      It's a dark eyed sailor that's proving my downfall."

3. "It's two long years since he left the land,
   He took a gold ring from off my hand,
   We broke the token, here's part with me,
   And the other lies rolling,
   And the other lies rolling at the bottom of the sea."

4. Then half the ring did young William show,
   She was distracted midst joy and woe,
   "Oh, welcome, Wiliam, I've lands and gold,
   For my dark eyed sailor,
   For my dark eyed sailor, so manly, true and bold."

5. Then in a village down by the sea
   They joined in wedlock and well agree;
   So maids be true while your love's away,
   For a cloudy morning,
   For a cloudy morning brings forth a shining day.

62051

III. THE DARK EYED SAILOR

PRESENTATION: This ballad, like "Where are you going to, my pretty maid?" may be presented simply, with the three necessary characters, or with two or more sets of sailors and comely maidens. The following plan has been worked out for two sets of players, with choral singing and silent pantomime. (The actions of each set must be in strict unison.)

STAGING: No properties are required; the stage represents a beach at the seaside, and later a village church.

COSTUMING: Eighteenth century costumes add quaintness to this production. The girls should look as simple as possible, with perhaps, sunbonnets, and dresses with puff-sleeves. The sailors are English jack-tars of the day-before-yesterday, and may even sport pigtails. The parson should wear some dignified-looking robe, and a clerical hat.

ACTION: The action must be lively and the singing spirited.

VERSE 1.
> *It was a comely young lady fair,*

The maidens enter from stage L., one after the other, strolling coyly. The sailors enter from stage R., also in single file, passing behind the maidens, and casting arch glances at them. The men walk in sprightly fashion. Everybody takes five steps.

> *Was walking out for to take the air;*

They now turn, and walk in the opposite direction for five steps, the sailors showing interest, the girls looking demure.

> *She met a sailor all on her way,*

They repeat the walk, as in line 1.

> *So I paid attention,*

The maidens stand expectantly. The sailors compare notes about the girls, and decide on a course of action.

THE DARK EYED SAILOR

So I paid attention to what they did say.

Choosing the maiden nearer him, each sailor steps up to her and bows, while she curtsies. The four are now standing in a row: girl, sailor, sailor, girl, with a space between the two couples.

VERSE 2.

Said William, "Lady, why walk alone?
The night is coming and the day near gone."

The sailors entreat, indicating the coming of night. The maids cast down their eyes modestly.

She said, while tears from her eyes did fall,

The maidens begin to weep. The sailors look on.

"It's a dark eyed sailor,
It's a dark eyed sailor that's proving my downfall."

The maidens wring their hands, then gaze romantically into space. The sailors dance a few steps of the hornpipe.

VERSE 3.

"It's two long years since he left the land,
He took a gold ring from off my hand,
We broke the token, here's part with me,

The girls pantomime the length of time they have been alone. They demonstrate the removal of the ring and the breaking of it; then they bring their keepsakes from round their necks.

And the other lies rolling,
And the other lies rolling at the bottom of the sea."

The maids indicate the position of the other halves at the bottom of the sea. The sailors exchange artful glances, listening knowingly to the girls throughout the verse, and even taking the audience into their confidence with a deliberate wink!

VERSE 4.

Then half the ring did young William show,

37

THE DARK EYED SAILOR

The sailors produce dramatically their tokens from their hip-
pockets.

She was distracted midst joy and woe,

The girls show extreme joy, followed by woe. (They might give a
couple of jumps with expressions of delight, and then suddenly assume a drooping attitude with their hands to their eyes.)

"Oh, welcome, William, I've lands and gold,

The maidens embrace the sailors, and pantomime their comfortable
financial situation.

For my dark eyed sailor,
For my dark eyed sailor, so manly, true and bold."

Each maiden skips around, hand in hand with her sailor.

VERSE 5.

Then in a village down by the sea

The parson enters back centre, with deliberately dignified steps,
and takes up a position upstage centre, facing the audience. The
sailors lead their girls up to him. The four kneel on the last note of
the line, with their backs to the audience, each couple a little to the
side of the parson.

They joined in wedlock and well agree;

The sailors put rings on the maidens' fingers on the second syllable
of the word "wedlock." They all stand up as the parson blesses
them with a gesture.

So maids be true while your love's away,

The couples kiss, hold hands, and gaze admiringly at one another.

For a cloudy morning,
For a cloudy morning brings forth a shining day.

They skip round and round the stage, dancing off, one couple to R.,
one to L. The parson walks out solemnly, as the music ends.

38

IV. *DASHING AWAY WITH A SMOOTHING IRON*

IV. DASHING AWAY WITH A
SMOOTHING IRON

Moderato

Englis

1- 'Twas on a Mon - day morn - ing, When

I be - held my darl - ing, She

look'd so neat and charm - - - ing In

ev - 'ry high de - - - gree She

look'd so neat and nim - ble O A -

wash - ing of her lin - en O,

Dash - ing a - way with a smooth - ing iron,

Dash - ing a - way with a smooth - ing iron, She

last verse

stole my heart a - - way, wa - -ay!

IV. DASHING AWAY WITH A
SMOOTHING IRON

2. 'Twas on a Tuesday morning,
   When I beheld my darling,
   She look'd so neat and charming
   In ev'ry high degree,
   She look'd so neat and nimble-O
   A-hanging of her linen-O,
   Dashing away, etc.

3. 'Twas on a Wednesday morning,
   When I beheld my darling,
   She look'd so neat and charming
   In ev'ry high degree,
   She look'd so neat and nimble-O
   A-starching of her linen-O,
   Dashing away, etc.

4. 'Twas on a Thursday morning,
   When I beheld my darling,
   She look'd so neat and charming
   In ev'ry high degree,
   She look'd so neat and nimble-O
   An-ironing of her linen-O,
   Dashing away, etc.

5. 'Twas on a Friday morning,
   When I beheld my darling,
   She look'd so neat and charming
   In ev'ry high degree,
   She look'd so neat and nimble-O
   An-airing of her linen-O,
   Dashing away, etc.

6. 'Twas on a Saturday morning,
   When I beheld my darling,
   She look'd so neat and charming
   In ev'ry high degree,
   She look'd so neat and nimble-O
   A-folding of her linen-O,
   Dashing away, etc.

7. 'Twas on a Sunday morning,
   When I beheld my darling,
   She look'd so neat and charming
   In ev'ry high degree,
   She look'd so neat and nimble-O
   A-wearing of her linen-O,
   Dashing away, etc.

IV. DASHING AWAY WITH A SMOOTHING IRON

PRESENTATION: This ballad is unusual since it requires only one character. A soloist, or a chorus, sings the song, while the girl pantomimes the action.

STAGING: Realistic treatment is almost obligatory, as so much of the action centres around homely tasks. In the middle of the stage is a table, on which are a wash-tub, a small bowl, a scrubbing board, a flat iron, and several pieces of underwear. Besides these there should be a dress which resembles that worn by the girl in verse 7. Suspended diagonally across the right side of the stage is a clothes line; at back centre, a fire-place with a screen in front, and a stool to one side of it.

COSTUMING: The girl wears a pretty chintz pinafore which completely covers the dress she has beneath it. This dress is in the "Kate Greenaway" style, perhaps of voile or organdie, very dainty in type.

ACTION: There is little "drama" in this ballad. Its charm lies in its gaiety, and the rhythmic execution of all the young girl's simple tasks. She should move lightly about her work, exaggerating her gestures to make them the more effective. Till verse 7 the singing is gay and rather quick.

VERSE 1.

> *'Twas on a Monday morning*
> *When I beheld my darling,*

The girl enters from L. She takes seven steps across to the table, and stands behind it, facing the audience.

DASHING AWAY

She look'd so neat and charming
In ev'ry high degree,

She picks up and tosses into the wash-tub the clothes to be laundered, using first one hand and then the other, for four counts.

She look'd so neat and nimble-O
A-washing of her linen-O,
Dashing away, etc.

She imitates rubbing clothes on the scrub board, which is inside the wash-tub, using ten large gestures.

VERSE 2.

'Twas on a Tuesday morning
When I beheld my darling,

She picks up the wash-tub, takes five steps over to the clothes-line, and deposits the tub on the floor.

She look'd so neat and charming
In ev'ry high degree,
She look'd so neat and nimble-O
A-hanging of her linen-O

She picks the clothes from the tub, and hangs them over the line, moving rhythmically. She surveys them with satisfaction.

Dashing away, etc.

She holds out her skirts and dances happily about the stage, ending beside the clothes-line.

VERSE 3.

'Twas on a Wednesday morning
When I beheld my darling,

She takes the clothes off the line, piling them in her arms.

WITH A SMOOTHING IRON

She look'd so neat and charming
In ev'ry high degree,

She takes five steps back to the table, placing the clothing upon it.

She look'd so neat and nimble-O

She separates the various articles.

A-starching of her linen-O,
Dashing away, etc.

She pantomimes starching them, using the bowl as the starch-container.

VERSE 4.

'Twas on a Thursday morning
When I beheld my darling,
She look'd so neat and charming
In ev'ry high degree,

Rhythmically she smoothes the clothes, laying them flat on the table.

She look'd so neat and nimble-O
An-ironing of her linen-O,
Dashing away, etc.

Seizing the flat-iron she vigorously presses the clothes with large, sweeping gestures, laying down the iron at the end of the refrain.

VERSE 5.

During this verse, she holds up each article of clothing, then takes it to the fireplace where she lays it over the screen, repeating the process until the end of the verse and refrain. She remains by the fireplace ready for the action in verse 6.

45

DASHING AWAY

'Twas on a Saturday morning
When I beheld my darling,
She look'd so neat and charming
In ev'ry high degree,
She look'd so neat and nimble-O
A-folding of her linen-O,

She folds the clothes, piling them neatly on the stool, using rhythmic gestures.

Dashing away with a smoothing iron,
She lifts the pile, holds it at arms' length, and smiles contentedly.

Dashing away, etc.
She goes off L., taking seven skipping steps.

VERSE 7.

'Twas on a Sunday morning
When I beheld my darling
She quickly removes the pinafore, *offstage*, dons a bonnet, ready to re-appear wearing the pretty dress similar to that in the "washing." (The singing of lines 1–6 is very slow and deliberate.)

She look'd so neat and charming
In ev'ry high degree,
She look'd so neat and nimble-O
A-wearing of her linen-O,

She re-enters L., walking slowly, with eyes downcast, palms devoutly pressed together. She takes eight steps across the stage.

Dashing away, etc.
Suddenly her mood changes. The singers speed up the tempo and she dances merrily round the stage, taking twelve skipping steps. She waves her hand to the audience on the last note of the music as she disappears offstage R.

46

V. *THE DUMB WIFE CURED*

V. THE DUMB WIFE CURED

Quickly and liltingly　　　　　　　　　　　　　　　　English

1- There was a bon - ny blade Had

mar - ried a coun - try maid And

safe - - - ly con - duct - ed her

Home, home, home; She was

neat in ev - 'ry part, And she

pleased him to the heart, But

ah, a - - - las, she was Dumb, dumb, dumb.

V. THE DUMB WIFE CURED

2. She was bright as the day,
   And as brisk as the May,
   And as round and as plump as a
   Plum, plum, plum;
   But still the silly swain
   Could do nothing but complain
   Because that his wife was
   Dumb, dumb, dumb.

3. She could brew, she could bake,
   She could sew and she could make,
   She could sweep the house with a
   Broom, broom, broom;
   She could wash and she could wring,
   Could do any kind of thing,
   But, ah, alas, she was
   Dumb, dumb, dumb.

4. To the doctor then he went
   For to give himself content,
   And to cure his wife of the
   Mum, mum, mum:
   "Oh, it is the easiest part
   That belongs unto my art,
   For to make a woman speak that is
   Dumb, dumb, dumb."

5. To the doctor he did her bring
   And he cut her chatt'ring string,
   And at liberty he set her
   Tongue, tongue, tongue;

Her tongue began to walk,
And she began to talk
As though she had never been
Dumb, dumb, dumb.

6. Her faculty she tried
And she filled the house with noise,
And she rattled in his ears like a
Drum, drum, drum:
She bred a deal of strife,
Made him weary of his life,
He'd give anything again she was
Dumb, dumb, dumb.

7. To the doctor then he goes
And thus he vents his woes,
"Oh, doctor, you've me un-
Done, done, done,
For my wife she's turned a scold,
And her tongue can never hold,
I'd give any kind of thing she was
Dumb, dumb, dumb."

8. "When I did undertake
To make thy wife to speak,
It was a thing eas-i-ly
Done, done, done,
But 'tis past the art of man,
Let him do whate'er he can
For to make a scolding woman hold her
Tongue, tongue, tongue."

Reprinted from the Clarendon Song Book — 4, published by the Oxford University Press.

V. THE DUMB WIFE CURED

PRESENTATION: In this ballad perhaps the most effective method is to carry out the whole of the action in silent pantomime, to the accompaniment of choral singing.

STAGING: Stage R. represents the husband's house, stage L., the doctor's. On stage R. is a chair, on stage L., a table, on which may be a large bottle, marked POISON in bold letters, and several murderous-looking implements, such as a saw and a pair of shears; also on stage L. is a chair behind the table, facing the audience, and somewhere in the vicinity, a large black and white sign on which is painted a skull.

COSTUMING: This ballad, a characteristic satire upon the mediaeval shrew, should be costumed picturesquely, in some fashion typical of the Middle Ages. The wife should be padded, if necessary, in order to appear "as round and as plump as a plum."

ACTION: The action must be lively, the singing gay and the words particularly well enunciated.

VERSE 1.

> *There was a bonny blade*
> *Had married a country maid*
> *And safely conducted her*
> *Home, home, home;*

Enter from R. the "gallant blade" and his wife, holding hands, walking gaily to the centre of the stage, in time with the music. Enter from L. the doctor, solemnly, who seats himself at his table, opens a large book he is carrying, and begins to read.

> *She was neat in ev'ry part,*

The wife curtsies; the husband bows.

And she pleased him to the heart,

They embrace.

But ah, alas, she was
Dumb, dumb, dumb.

She wrings her hands, and bows her head. He looks discouraged and turns from her.

VERSE 2.

She was bright as the day,
And as brisk as the May,

The wife takes the husband's hands and they dance round together; he sits in the chair on the word "May."

And as round and as plump as a
Plum, plum, plum;

She pirouettes round and round, trying to get his attention. He looks away, very much displeased.

But still the silly swain
Could do nothing but complain
Because that his wife she was
Dumb, dumb, dumb.

She drops curtsies to him, looks appealingly at him, pantomimes great distress, and wrings her hands. He sits with a discontented look on his face.

VERSE 3.

She could brew, she could bake,

She pantomimes brewing and baking.

She could sew and she could make,

She pantomimes sewing.

THE DUMB WIFE CURED

> *She could sweep the house with a*
> *Broom, broom, broom;*

She pantomimes sweeping the room.

> *She could wash and she could wring,*

She pantomimes washing and wringing.

> *Could do any kind of thing.*

She pantomimes her ability to do everything.

> *But, ah, alas, she was*
> *Dumb, dumb, dumb.*

She wrings her hands, looking downcast. The husband sits stolidly throughout the verse.

VERSE 4.

> *To the doctor then he went*
> *For to give himself content,*
> *And to cure his wife of the*

The husband rises, walks to the doctor's house, and raps on the table rhythmically for attention; the wife seats herself in the chair vacated by her spouse, crosses her feet, folds her hands, and looks into space for the rest of the verse.

> *Mum, mum, mum:*

The husband points to the wife, indicating that she is dumb.

> *"Oh, it is the easiest part*
> *That belongs unto my art,*
> *For to make a woman speak that is*
> *Dumb, dumb, dumb."*

The doctor, indicates, in pantomime, his ability to cure her.

VERSE 5.

> *To the doctor he did her bring*

The husband goes to his wife, and quickly brings her to the doctor.

53

THE DUMB WIFE CURED

And he cut her chatt'ring string.

The doctor rhythmically pantomimes cutting the woman's tongue. He may at the same time make a rasping sound, imitative of the noise of a saw! She looks aghast, but sticks out her tongue for the operation.

> *And at liberty he set her*
> *Tongue, tongue, tongue;*

Both men look at her. She registers extreme joy. She lets out a great burst of talk (in pantomime, of course!).

> *Her tongue began to walk,*
> *And she began to talk*
> *As though she had never been*
> *Dumb, dumb, dumb.*

The wife continues to show great joy, keeps on chattering, kisses the doctor and her husband, while the latter is paying for the treatment. (Here, if a violinist is available, it affords an amusing touch if he produces a long drawn-out squawk at the end of the verse while the wife pantomimes screeching at the top of her lungs.)

VERSE 6.

> *Her faculty she tried*

The husband conducts his wife home. She continues to talk delightedly.

> *And she filled the house with noise,*

She sits; he regards her.

> *And she rattled in his ears like a*
> *Drum, drum, drum:*
> *She bred a deal of strife,*
> *Made him weary of his life,*
> *He'd give anything again she was*
> *Dumb, dumb, dumb.*

THE DUMB WIFE CURED

She makes faces, laughs, scolds, screams in silent pantomime. The husband holds his ears, looking amazed and horrified.

VERSE 7.

> *To the doctor then he goes*
> *And thus he vents his woes,*

The wife continues her tantrums; the husband goes back to the doctor's place, and knocks on the table.

> *"O doctor you've me un-*
> *Done, done, done,*
> *For my wife she's turned a scold,*
> *And her tongue can never hold,*
> *I'd give any kind of thing she was*
> *Dumb, dumb, dumb."*

He complains of his wife, who continues talking to herself. The doctor listens thoughtfully.

VERSE 8.

> *"When I did undertake*

The wife rises, and walks over to take part in the discussion, chattering triumphantly, while the doctor begins his explanation.

> *To make thy wife to speak,*
> *It was a thing easily*

The doctor reasons with the husband.

> *Done, done, done,*

The wife yells in her husband's ear, making him jump in agony.

> *But 'tis past the art of man,*
> *Let him do whate'er he can*
> *For to make a scolding woman hold her*
> *Tongue tongue, tongue."*

THE DUMB WIFE CURED

The doctor signifies his inability to rectify matters; the wife takes her husband off R., holding his ear and screaming into it; the husband grabs the poison bottle before his undignified exit; the doctor addresses himself in pantomime to the audience as he leaves L., walking slowly, shaking his head. (A prolonged wail from the violin!)

VI. *THE GOLDEN GLOVE*

VI. THE GOLDEN GLOVE

Moderato   English

1—A weal - thy young squire - of Tam - worth we hear, He court - ed a no - ble - man's daugh - ter so fair; To mar - ry this la - - dy it was his in - - tent, All friends and re - - la - - tions gave glad - ly con - sent.

VI. THE GOLDEN GLOVE

2. The time was appointed for their wedding day,
   A young farmer chosen to give her away;
   As soon as the farmer this lady did spy,
   He inflamèd her heart; "Oh my heart!" she did cry.

3. She turned from the squire, but nothing she said;
   Instead of being married she took to her bed;
   The thought of the farmer ran sore in her mind,
   A way to secure him she quickly did find.

4. Coat, waistcoat, and breeches she then did put on,
   And a-hunting she went with her dog and her gun;
   She hunted around where the farmer did dwell,
   Because in her heart she did love him full well.

5. She oftentimes fired, but nothing she killed,
   At length the young farmer came into the field;
   And as to discourse with him was her intent,
   With her dog and her gun to meet him she went.

6. "I thought you had been at the wedding," she cried,
   "To wait on the squire, and give him his bride."
   "No, sir," said the farmer, "if the truth I may tell,
   I'll not give her away, for I love her too well."

7. "Suppose that the lady should grant you her love?
   You know that the squire your rival would prove."
   "Why, then," says the farmer, "with sword-blade in hand,
   By honor I'll gain her when she shall command."

8. It pleasèd the lady to find him so bold;
   She gave him a glove that was flowered with gold,
   And she told him she found it when coming along,
   As she was a-hunting with dog and with gun.

9. The lady went home with a heart full of love,
   And she gave out a notice that she'd lost a glove;
   And said, "Who has found it, and brings it to me,
   Whoever he is, he my husband shall be."

10. The farmer was pleased when he heard of the news,
    With heart full of joy to the lady he goes.
    "Dear honored lady, I've picked up your glove,
    And hope you'll be pleasèd to grant me your love."

11. "It already is granted, and I'll be your bride;
    I love the sweet breath of a farmer," she cried,
    "I'll be mistress of dairy, and milking the cow,
    While my jolly brisk farmer sings shrill at the plough."

12. And when she was married she told of her fun,
    And how she went a-hunting with dog and with gun.
    "And now I have got him so fast in my snare,
    I'll enjoy him for ever, I vow and declare."

VI. THE GOLDEN GLOVE

PRESENTATION: So much lively dialogue occurs in this ballad that the players should say their lines, or better, sing them. A chorus sings the narrative.

STAGING: The stage must represent the nobleman's castle, and the farmer's lands, so should be perfectly empty, the imagination furnishing the necessary settings.

COSTUMING: Eighteenth century costumes are appropriate. The squire and the relatives wear rich apparel, so does the lady except when in disguise; then she dons a coat, waistcoat, breeches and cap, and carries a little gun. The farmer wears a smock and breeches, the parson a long black cloak and "shovel" hat, the town-crier may wear a cocked hat and carry a bell.

ACTION: Most of the charm of this dramatization depends upon the actress who interprets the lady's part, especially in the scene where she masquerades. She may facilitate her change of costume, during lines 3 and 4 of verse 3, by wearing breeches and waistcoat under her dress from the start of the play.

VERSE 1.
      A wealthy young squire of Tamworth we hear,
The young lady enters from right, accompanied by her mother. They are followed by friends and relatives and the young farmer who stands downstage right. They walk in rhythm with the music, the lady and her mother taking seven steps on to the stage, the others grouping themselves around them, but not in front of them. The squire enters from the left, and takes seven steps over to the lady and her mother.

      He courted a nobleman's daughter so fair;
The squire kisses the mother's hand, then the young lady's.

THE GOLDEN GLOVE

To marry this lady it was his intent

He kneels before her on the first syllable of "marry," places his right hand on his heart on the first syllable of "lady," then extends the same hand towards her in entreaty on "was."

All friends and relations gave gladly consent.

Everyone looks pleased, excepting the young lady, who turns slightly from the squire, and casts down her eyes. He rises from his knees, and has his hand shaken by the mother and a male relative who steps up beside him. Other friends pat him on the back, rhythmically. Two female relatives kiss the girl effusively.

VERSE 2.

The time was appointed for their wedding day,

The parson enters from L., taking seven dignified steps across to left of centre.

A young farmer chosen to give her away;

The mother beckons to the farmer, who takes three strides over to the daughter and stands on the right of her.

As soon as the farmer this lady did spy,

The squire preens himself in anticipation, the minor characters converse (silently), but the daughter and the farmer look into each other's eyes, and stand quite still.

He inflamèd her heart; "Oh my heart!" she did cry.

The lady places her right hand on her heart, and whispers, "Oh, my heart," as she continues to gaze at the farmer. Her mother gives place to the squire, who takes two proud steps over to his fiancee, produces a ring from his pocket, and holds it out to her.

VERSE 3.

She turned from the squire, but nothing she said;

THE GOLDEN GLOVE

The girl refuses the ring with a sweeping gesture, and, turning her back, takes two steps upstage. Great consternation is shown by all present, particularly by the squire who clenches his fists and frowns. The parson raises shocked hands to heaven.

Instead of being married she took to her bed;

The mother puts her arms round her swooning daughter, and assists her out, right. The squire, his face convulsed with rage, takes three steps downstage to the left, occupying an isolated position. The farmer looks solicitously after the departing figure of the young lady. All the relatives continue to compare notes, and to gossip in groups. The parson stands bewildered.

The thought of the farmer ran sore in her mind,
A way to secure him she quicky did find.

They all go off left at different rates of speed: the parson shaking his head vigorously, the squire proudly, nose in air, the relatives in great perturbation, and the farmer looking back regretfully.

Verse 4.

Coat, waistcoat, and breeches she then did put on,

The lady enters from R., carrying a gun; she wears a cap, coat, waistcoat and breeches. She takes three mannish strides on to the stage, then stands smiling to herself, inspectng her garments and assuming a masculine swagger.

And a-hunting she went with her dog and her gun;

She walks about the stage for eight steps, as if spying, looking expectantly from side to side.

She hunted around where the farmer did dwell,

She pantomimes firing two shots into the air in different directions on the words "hunted" and "farmer," gazing eagerly to the left between shots.

THE GOLDEN GLOVE

Because in her heart she did love him full well.

On the second syllable of "because" she rests the butt of her gun on the ground, places her left hand on her heart on the word "heart." On the word "love" she reaches out that hand towards the left, looking longingly into the distance, and on "well" she replaces her hand on her heart.

VERSE 5.

She oftentimes fired, but nothing she killed,

Walking towards the right she fires four random shots with her gun, in time with the music. Her back is towards the farmer when he enters L.

At length the young farmer came into the field;

The farmer walks in a circle round the left side of the stage, pantomiming sowing seed. He keeps this up until the end of the verse, unconscious of the lady, who turns, lowers her gun, and gazes at him with admiration.

And as to discourse with him was her intent,

She puts her gun under her left arm on the word "as," pulls her cap well over her eyes on "discourse," looks out at the audience roguishly, wagging her right forefinger at them twice in time with the music.

With her dog and her gun to meet him she went.

She takes five strides over to the farmer, standing still and observing him during the last three beats of the line. He sees her and stops his work.

VERSE 6.

"I thought you had been at the wedding," she cried,

As she speaks to him she points to the right. Throughout her con-

versation with him she makes her gestures with her right hand;
she holds her gun in her left.

> *To wait on the squire and give him his bride."*

She turns from him and takes two mincing steps to the right,
darting a mischievous glance at the farmer, as she pantomimes
"giving away," with a large gesture from left to right. He listens,
and watches her, with a pained expression on his face.

> *"No, sir," said the farmer, "if the truth I may tell,*

The farmer takes a step after her, his fists clenched. She turns her
head away from him and smiles happily.

> *I'll not give her away, for I love her too well."*

The farmer shakes his head, places his hand on his heart and looks
romantically into space.

VERSE 7.

> *"Suppose that the lady should grant you her love?*

The lady assumes a jaunty air, looking roguishly into the farmer's
face as she holds out her right hand to him. He listens and watches
her.

> *You know that the squire your rival would prove."*

She pantomimes drawing a sword, flourishing it in the air and
thrusting it at the farmer on the word "prove."

> *"Why then," says the farmer, "with sword-blade in hand,*

As he replies, the farmer also pantomimes drawing a sword.

> *By honor I'll gain her when she shall command."*

Striking a heroic attitude he stands, right arm upstretched, left
hand on his heart. She gazes at him admiringly, her hand clasped to
her heart.

THE GOLDEN GLOVE

> *It pleasèd the lady to find him so bold;*

Overcome by his emotion he turns his back to the audience, takes four strides upstage, folds his arms and stands still. She watches him, smiles joyfully, and pulls the glove from her pocket, looking first at it, then at the farmer, with a twinkle in her eye.

> *She gave him a glove that was flowered with gold,*

She takes a few quick steps over to him, and taps him on the shoulder on "glove." He turns and faces her, examining the glove which she puts in his hand.

> *And she told him she found it when coming along,*

She points back in the direction from which she has come, retracing three steps of her earlier movements, in explanation, over to the right.

> *As she was a-hunting with dog and with gun.*

She pantomimes shooting her gun four times into the air.

Verse 9.

> *The lady went home with a heart full of love,*

The farmer goes off L., looking back in bewilderment at the "hunter," then at the glove which he carries. The lady walks off R. Both move to the rhythm of the music. (The lady must quickly resume her feminine garb.)

> *And she gave out a notice that she'd lost a glove;*
> *And said, "Who has found it, and brings it to me,*
> *Whoever he is, he my husband shall be."*

The town-crier struts in R., followed by a crowd (the men and women of the first three verses). He goes to the centre of the stage. The people group themselves round him, peering at the proclamation he holds out for their inspection, and from which he shouts (silently) the lady's announcement. On the last line the lady enters

THE GOLDEN GLOVE

from right as the farmer enters from left. Each takes four steps across the stage towards the crowd.

The farmer was pleased when he heard of the news,
Joyfully the farmer takes the glove from his pocket, holds it at arm's length, and surveys it delightedly. The lady stands watching him. The town-crier pursues his way across the stage to the left, disappearing during line 2. He is followed by the townspeople, who discuss the affair excitedly, but have not observed the farmer's actions.

With heart full of joy to the lady he goes:
The farmer takes seven steps over to the lady.

"Dear honored lady I've picked up your glove,
He bows low, and hands her the glove.

And hope you'll be pleasèd to grant me your love."
He kneels, places his right hand on his heart, then extends it to her beseechingly. She looks down at him adoringly.

VERSE 11.

"It already is granted, and I'll be your bride;
Taking both his hands in hers, she raises him from his kneeling position; they embrace.

I love the sweet breath of a farmer," she cried,
With his right hand in her left they walk upstage together towards the centre. They take eight steps, turning to face the audience as the music of line 2 ends.

"I'll be mistress of dairy, and milking the cow,
While my jolly brisk farmer sings shrill at the plough."
While she says lines 3–4 her friends and relatives enter from either

side; they stand looking at her and the farmer, first with surprise, then with pleasure. The lady pantomimes milking a cow (line 3), and on line 4 she and the farmer join hands and skip round in a circle.

VERSE 12.

The lady and the farmer skip forward a few steps, turn their backs on the audience and join hands with all the relatives for a circular dance. On the last line of the verse the lady breaks the circle, and leads the company off, L. They all skip gaily out as the verse ends.

VII. *GOOD KING WENCESLAS*

VII. GOOD KING WENCESLAS

Christmas Carol

f

1—Good King Wen - ces - las look'd out.

On the Feast of Ste - phen, When the snow lay

round - a - bout, Deep, and crisp and ev - en:

Bright - ly shone the moon that night, Tho' the frost was

cru - el, When a poor man came in sight,

Gath - 'ring win - ter fu - - - - - - el.

VII. GOOD KING WENCESLAS

2. "Hither page, and stand by me,
   If thou know'st it telling,
   Yonder peasant, who is he?
   Where and what his dwelling?"
   "Sire, he lives a good league hence,
   Underneath the mountain;
   Right against the forest fence,
   By St. Agnes' fountain."

3. "Bring me flesh, and bring me wine,
   Bring me pine-logs hither;
   Thou and I will see him dine,
   When we bear them thither."
   Page and monarch forth they went,
   Forth they went together;
   Through the rude wind's wild lament
   And the bitter weather.

4. "Sire, the night is darker now,
   And the wind blows stronger;
   Fails my heart, I know not how,
   I can go no longer."
   "Mark my footsteps, good my page!
   Tread thou in them boldly:
   Thou shalt find the winter's rage
   Freeze thy blood less coldly."

GOOD KING WENCESLAS

5. In his master's steps he trod
   Where the snow lay dinted;
   Heat was in the very sod
   Which the Saint had printed.
   Therefore, Christian men, be sure,
   Wealth or rank possessing,
   Ye who now will bless the poor
   Shall yourselves find blessing.

VII. GOOD KING WENCESLAS

PRESENTATION: This Christmas carol, beloved for the picture it presents of human charity, has great dramatic possibilities. The utmost sincerity, however, must be contributed by singers and actors if the effect is to be completely satisfying. With sympathetic interpretation the result is one of extraordinary power, comparable to that produced by a mediaeval miracle play. The king and the page may sing their lines of dialogue, while the chorus carries the narrative.

STAGING: This may be elaborate, with the doorway of a mediaeval castle constructed on stage L and rich-looking wall hangings surrounding the rest of the stage; or it may be very simple, the left hand side of the stage representing the king's palace, the right being part of the royal domain. If possible, the effect should be given of snow, "deep and crisp and even." Several little Christmas trees stand on the right of the stage, glistening with frost and snow. From under these trees the "poor man" gathers his firewood. Imitation snow, procured from a Ten-Cent Store, sprinkled over the stage and on the trees, gives the necessary wintry effect. The lighting should, if possible, contribute to the seasonal atmosphere, cold moonlight flooding the scene from an offstage lamp. During verse 3 the page issues from the palace bearing a large basket containing provisions, and a bundle of faggots. A bottle of wine, prominently displayed, adds a festive touch.

COSTUMING: King Wenceslas has on a regal mediaeval robe, and a crown. He wears a patriarchal-looking beard. The page's garb is that of a fashionable boy of the Middle Ages. In contrast to the gorgeousness of the king's attire and the gaiety of the young page's, the drabness of the poverty-stricken peasant's rags is the more apparent.

GOOD KING WENCESLAS

ACTION: Great dignity characterizes the actions of Wenceslas. His gestures are expansive, his bearing noble. The page's movements are quick and sure, except towards the end of verse 3, and in verse 4. The peasant's shoulders are bowed; he appears feeble and dispirited.

VERSE 1.

> *Good King Wenceslas look'd out*
> *On the Feast of Stephen,*

The king appears at his doorway L. and gazes out at the snow-covered landscape.

> *When the snow lay round about,*
> *Deep, and crisp and even:*

He kneels in prayer.

> *Brightly shone the moon that night,*
> *Tho' the frost was cruel,*

The peasant enters from R. and begins gathering twigs from beneath the trees. He moves dejectedly, in time with the music, gradually approaching the centre of the stage. The king continues to kneel in prayer.

> *When a poor man came in sight,*
> *Gath'ring winter fuel.*

The peasant searches unsuccessfully for wood beneath the central tree. The King, rising from prayer, suddenly catches sight of him and watches him pityingly.

VERSE 2.

> *"Hither page, and stand by me,*

The king summons his page, with a gesture to L.

74

GOOD KING WENCESLAS

If thou know'st it telling,

The page appears from downstage L. on the word "if," and bows on the word "know'st."

Yonder peasant who is he ?
Where and what his dwelling ?"

The king, singing his lines, points to the peasant who has continued his task, wandering forlornly among the trees. The page looks at him, appearing to recognize him after some thought.

"Sire, he lives a good league hence,
Underneath the mountain;
Right against the forest fence,
By St. Agnes' fountain."

The page sings his reply, as he points off R. to the poor man's dwelling.

VERSE 3.

"Bring me flesh, and bring me wine,
Bring me pine-logs hither;

The king sings his commands; the page departs L. at the end of line 2. The peasant continues to forage.

Thou and I will see him dine,

Singing, the king looks over at the peasant.

When we bear them thither."

He continues to sing, the page returns, carrying the basket of provisions.

Page and monarch forth they went,
Forth they went together;
Through the rude wind's wild lament
And the bitter weather.

The king and the page step out of the doorway, walking abreast,

GOOD KING WENCESLAS

the page on the king's left. They walk slowly as if buffetted by a severe wind. The king takes seven sure steps, the page, after five steps, falters, almost loses his balance, retreats two steps, and stops.

VERSE 4.

> *"Sire, the night is darker now,*
>   *And the wind blows stronger;*
> *Fails my heart I know not how,*
>   *I can go no longer."*

The king turns to support the page, who lays down the basket as he sings. "Fails my heart," and sinks to the ground.

> *"Mark my footsteps, good my page!*
>   *Tread thou in them boldly:*
> *Thou shalt find the winter's rage*
>   *Freeze thy blood less coldly."*

The king helps the page to rise, lifts the basket himself, and turns to resume his journey.

VERSE 5.

> *In his master's steps he trod*
>   *Where the snow lay dinted;*
> *Heat was in the very sod*
>   *Which the Saint had printed.*

The page walks in his master's footsteps, gaining courage and strength from them. They take seven paces over to the peasant who is still gathering sticks over on the right.

> *Therefore, Christian men, be sure,*

The peasant removes his hat, kneels, and the king motions him to rise. The page stands looking on.

> *Wealth or rank possessing,*

The king presents the gift to the peasant.

GOOD KING WENCESLAS

Ye who now will bless the poor

The peasant shows great joy and gratitude. The king raises his hand to bless him.

Shall yourselves find blessing.

The poor man goes joyfully off R., carrying his basket. The king and the page exchange glances of pleasure as they watch his departure.

Conclusion: The chorus hums the last half of the melody, or as many measures as seem necessary for the king, followed by the page, to return to his castle and disappear within the doorway.

VIII. *GREEN BROOM*

VIII. GREEN BROOM

Rather slowly   English

1--There was an old man and he liv'd in the West, And his trade was a - cut - ting of broom, green broom; He had but one son and his name it was John, And he li - ed a - bed till 'twas noon, bright noon, And he li - ed a - bed till twas noon.

VIII. GREEN BROOM

2. The old man arose and unto his son goes,
   And he swore he'd set fire to his room, his room,
   If he would not rise and unbutton his eyes,
   And away to the woods for green broom, green broom.
   And away to the woods for green broom.

3. Then Jack he did rise and did sharpen his knives,
   And he went to the woods cutting broom, green broom,
   To market and fair, crying ev'rywhere,
   "O fair maids, do you want any broom, green broom?
   O fair maids, do you want any broom?"

4. A lady sat up in her window so high,
   And she heard Johnny crying "Green broom, green, broom;"
   She rang for her maid and unto her she said,
   "O go fetch me the lad that cries broom, green broom,
   O go fetch me the lad that cries broom."

5. Then John he came back, and upstairs he did go,
   And he enter'd that fair lady's room, her room,
   "Dear Johnny," said she, "O can you fancy me,
   Will you marry a lady in bloom, in bloom?
   Will you marry a lady in bloom?

6. Then John gave consent and unto the church went,
   And he married this lady in bloom, in bloom.
   Said she, "I protest there is none in the West
   Is so good as the lad who sells broom, green broom,
   Is so good as the lad who sells broom."

VIII. GREEN BROOM

PRESENTATION: A chorus sings the ballad, while the players mime the action. They may also say or sing their lines of dialogue, but, owing to the movements necessary in Verse 6, silent panto-mime seems most advisable.

STAGING: The old man's cottage is situated on the extreme left; the forest is in the centre of the stage; on the right, facing the audience, is a short flight of steps leading up to a little platform representing the lady's dwelling. (If necessary, however, her house may be on the same level as the wood and the cottage, imaginary steps being climbed in pantomime, to reach it.) A cot, with a chair near it, stands on stage left; on the platform, right, is a bench or chair; the old man and his son have large knives for their occupation; the lady has an embroidery frame.

COSTUMING: The young rustic is clad in a smock and breeches; his father has similar attire, though of more sombre hues. The lady wears an elegant-looking eighteenth century costume; her maid has a dress of the same period, an apron, and a mob cap. The country girls wear conventional milk-maids' costumes. The parson's attire includes a black cloak or coat, a clerical collar, a "shovel" hat, and spectacles.

ACTION: The mood of this ballad-play is jolly, and the charac-ters must take advantage of the humor inherent in their parts. The lazy boy, whose luck is out of all proportion to his merit, the long-suffering old father, the romantic and impulsive lady, and her obedient maid,— all should be played broadly, with exaggeration, and with animated facial expression on the part of the actors who portray them.

VERSE 1.

There was an old man and he liv'd in the West
And his trade was a-cutting of broom, green broom;

GREEN BROOM

The old man enters from L. followed by his son, John. The father takes seven steps to the centre of the stage, knife in hand, ready to begin work. John follows him on to the stage, takes three steps over to the bed, yawns, stretches, lies down, and goes off to sleep. The lady enters from R. She walks daintily for seven counts, and sits on her chair, on the last word of line 2.

He had but one son and his name it was John,
And he lièd a-bed till 'twas noon, bright noon,

The old man pantomimes cutting broom vigorously, in eight gestures. John breathes and snores in rhythm with the music. The lady sews busily, and rhythmically.

And he lièd a-bed till 'twas noon.

The action is the same for John and the lady as in lines 3–4.

The old man looks disgustedly over at his son, takes three strides over to him, and sits on the chair by the bed.

VERSE 2.

The old man arose and unto his son goes,

The old man stands up, and shakes John impatiently.

And he swore he'd set fire to his room, his room,

The son starts up, and gazes at his father in a dazed manner; the father shakes his fist at him, pantomimes striking a match, and applying it to the mattress of the bed.

If he would not rise and unbutton his eyes,

The old man shakes John twice, and tries to force his eyes open.

And away to the woods for green broom, green broom,

John is now awake, and thoroughly scared, as he watches his father gesticulate towards the woods, and pantomime the cutting of broom.

GREEN BROOM

And away to the woods for green broom.
The father goes off L., wagging his finger warningly at the son as
he disappears. John stares after him ruefully. Throughout the verse
the lady continues to sew.

VERSE 3.

Then Jack he did rise and did sharpen his knives,
John jumps out of bed, picks up his knife from the floor and
sharpens it on an imaginary carburundum.

And he went to the woods cutting broom, green broom,
He goes to the woods, in four determined strides.

To market and fair, crying ev'rywhere,
He pantomimes vigorously cutting broom. Village maidens come
tripping on to the stage from the right, they stand around watching
him admiringly.

"O fair maids, do you want any broom, green broom?
He offers the broom with his most engaging smiles. They buy it
with alacrity.

O fair maids, do you want any broom?"
They run off R., laughing, and waving him goodbye. He gazes after
them romantically as they disappear. The lady continues to sew.

VERSE 4.

A lady sat up in her window so high,
And she heard Johnny crying "Green broom, green broom;"
John pantomimes loading his back with broom; he walks about, and,
with hand to mouth, pantomimes shouting "Green Broom" to right
and to left. The lady listens, stands up, and peeps at him through an
imaginary window.

84

GREEN BROOM

She rang for her maid and unto her she said,
The lady puts down her embroidery on the chair, gives two vigorous pulls at an imaginary bell-rope, the maid runs in from R., bobs on the word "said," and stands at the bottom of the steps, looking up attentively at her mistress.

"O go fetch me the lad that cries broom, green broom,
The lady points longingly at John (who continues to walk about, calling his trade), then lays her hand romantically on her heart.

O go fetch me the lad that cries broom."
The maid runs over to John, taking seven steps. The lady repeats the action of line 4.

VERSE 5.

Then John he came back, and upstairs he did go,
And he enter'd that fair lady's room, her room,
On the word "then" the maid takes the bewildered Johnny's right hand and points up to her mistress. Together they cross the stage, ascend the stairs and approach the lady, each taking seven steps. John is between the lady and her maid.

"Dear Johnny," said she, "O can you fancy me?
John gazes at the lady in admiration. She looks at him, entranced, and clasps her hands together in entreaty. The maid listens in amazement. Her jaw drops when she hears the word "fancy." John shows pleasure and surprise.

Will you marry a lady in bloom, in bloom?
The lady holds out her arms to John on the word "marry." On the first "bloom" she places her right forefinger under her chin, supporting her right elbow on the back of her left hand, and curtsies. The maid raises her hands and eyes in astonishment, on the word "marry," and on the first "bloom," places her arms akimbo. John

stands quite still, puzzled, and yet pleased at the unexpected turn of events.

> *Will you marry a lady in bloom ?"*

The same as for line 4.

VERSE 6.

> *Then John gave consent and unto the church went,*
> *And he married this lady in bloom, in bloom.*

The parson enters from R. with hands clasped in front of him; he takes five steps across the stage, and stands to the L. of the steps, facing the audience. John nods his head decisively on the words "John" and "consent"; he takes the lady's right hand in his left. Together they walk down the steps and across the stage, taking up positions in front of the parson, facing him. Each takes six steps. The maid descends the stairs behind the couple, showing great surprise and interest. At the end of the music of line 2 she will have taken four steps, so, during line 3 she must continue across the stage, taking up a position on the lady's left hand, facing the parson.

> *Said she, "I protest there is none in the West*

On the word "she," John and the lady kneel. On the second syllable of "protest," the parson hands John a ring. John places it on the lady's finger, on the word "none." Both rise and face each other. The maid shows keen interest. At the beginning of the line the village maidens return from R., holding their skirts out and skipping lightly across the stage in single file behind the parson.

> *Is so good as the lad who sells broom, green broom,*

The village maids skip round the marriage group, who join hands; parson, bride, groom, and maid, dance round in a circle, in time with the music. The outer circle of villagers goes in contrary motion. The father enters L., takes two steps, and stands thunderstruck, unnoticed by the revellers.

GREEN BROOM

Is so good as the lad who sells broom."
The village maids go off R. skipping, in single file, turning to wave at the chief characters as they make their exit. The principals continue to dance; mouth open, the father throws his hat on the ground on the word "good," registering his amazement.

Conclusion: While the chorus repeat the last two lines, the bride and groom dance off R. The father goes off L. on the second line of the "repeat," shaking his head at the irony of Fate, and making a gesture indicative of complete bafflement.

IX. *MY LADY GREENSLEEVES*

IX. MY LADY GREENSLEEVES

English

Introduction (repeat between verses 3 & 4 - twice at end)

1—A -
las! my love, you do me wrong To
cast me off dis - court - - - eous - ly, And
I have lov - - - ed you so long, De -
light - - ing in your com - pan - y. *Chorus:* For
oh, Green - sleeves was all my joy, And
oh, Green - sleeves was my de - light And
oh, Green sleeves was my heart of gold, And
who but my la - - - - - dy Green - sleeves.

IX. MY LADY GREENSLEEVES

2. I bought thee kerchers to thy head
   That were wrought fine and gallantly;
   I kept thee booth at board and bed,
   Which cost my purse well favoredly.
   For, oh, Greensleeves, etc.

3. Thy smock of silk, both faire and white,
   With gold embroidered gorgeously:
   Thy petticoat of sendal right;
   And these I bought thee gladly.
   For, oh, Greensleeves, etc.

4. Greensleeves, now farewell, adieu,
   God I pray to prosper thee !
   For I am still thy lover true,
   Come once again and love me !
   For, oh, Greensleeves, etc.

IX. MY LADY GREENSLEEVES

PRESENTATION: An interpretation of the mood, rather than of the content of this ballad has been attempted in the following scheme. In a ballad which has beauty comparable to that of "Greensleeves," but which contains relatively little action, such treatment is often more interesting than the literal method.

A chorus sings while the players enact the scene; a fiddler supplies the introductory music and accompanies the song.

STAGING: No scenery or stage properties are necessary, though the charm of this ballad is intensified if the lighting effects are artistic, and if richly colored hangings are used, to give a mediaeval background.

COSTUMING: The costumes should be as gorgeous as possible. "Greensleeves" wears an elaborate mediaeval gown, with long green sleeves which almost touch the floor, and a "steeple" hat, draped with chiffon; the two young knights are also attired in clothes of the period, one carries a richly embroidered scarf, the other a gilded jewel-casket.

ACTION: To show the fickleness of Greensleeves, two suitors are introduced, with whom she coquettes, playing one off against the other, finally deserting both. Every movement must be absolutely rhythmic.

VERSE 1.

> *Alas! my love, you do me wrong*
> *To cast me off discourteously,*

Enter Greensleeves from upstage R, walking coyly, holding her skirt; she takes eleven steps (during the musical introduction and the first two lines of the song), going to the centre, downstage.

> *And I have lovèd you so long,*

She looks off-stage L. shading her eyes with her hand, as if in search of someone; she repeats this to R.

MY LADY GREENSLEEVES

Delighting in your company.

She walks backwards for three steps, folds her hands, lowers her
eyes coyly, and stands quite still.

Chorus.

> *For oh, Greensleeves, etc.*

Enter first suitor from R. second suitor from L. carrying their
gifts. They cross the stage, passing each other en route, and
stand on either side of Greensleeves. The suitors may, instead of
walking in the usual manner, make their movements stylized, taking three sprightly steps forward and one step back, for fifteen
counts. They hold their gifts with extended arms. Greensleeves
stands motionless, eyes downcast.

Verse 2.

> *I bought thee kerchers to thy head*

The first suitor kneels on the word "bought" and holds out the scarf
to Greensleeves on the word "to."

> *That were wrought fine and gallantly;*

Greensleeves makes a gesture of refusal with her hands on the
word "were," the first suitor, on the word "gallantly," sinks back
on the ground, disappointed at her treatment of him and his gift.

> *I kept thee booth at board and bed,*

The second suitor offers his gift, as did the first suitor in line 1.

> *Which cost my purse well favoredly.*

Greensleeves refuses his gift and he reacts in a fashion similar to
that of the first suitor. The same rhythm is maintained throughout.

Chorus.

> *For oh, Greensleeves was all my joy,*
> *And oh, Greensleeves was my delight,*

Greensleeves, taking eight steps, walks in a circle round the first
suitor who remains dejectedly on the floor. He catches the end
of her sleeve, kisses it and follows Greensleeves with his eyes.

MY LADY GREENSLEEVES

> *And oh, Greensleeves was my heart of gold,*
> *And who but my lady Greensleeves.*

Greensleeves, taking seven steps, walks in a circle round the second suitor, who behaves in similar fashion to the first suitor in lines 1–2. Greensleeves stands quietly between the two young men, with arms outspread, as the chorus ends.

VERSE 3.

> *Thy smock of silk, both faire and white,*

The suitors rise, with their backs to the audience; each lifts one of the lady's sleeves, and looks at her adoringly. They both take three short steps upstage, and one step back. (The gifts are left on the ground.) Greensleeves stands motionless.

> *With gold embroidered gorgeously;*

They repeat the dance step of line 1., looking back at the lady and relinquishing her sleeves on the last syllable of "gorgeously."

> *Thy petticoat of sendal right;*
> *And these I bought thee gladly.*

Greensleeves takes seven steps away from the suitors (who have dropped her sleeves), and to the right, standing motionless and with inscrutable expression. The suitors stand watching her departure with dismay during the third line, then take three steps towards one another, stand back to back, each pointing the "downstage" foot and bowing his head dejectedly on the the last syllable of "gladly."

Chorus.

> *For oh, Greensleeves was all my joy,*

Greensleeves suddenly smiles dazzlingly, takes four steps upstage in the direction of the second suitor, and throws him a kiss. He cannot believe his eyes.

MY LADY GREENSLEEVES

And oh, Greensleeves was my delight,

She continues on her way for four more steps, passing behind the two men, and throws a kiss to the first suitor, who is equally gratified.

And oh, Greensleeves was my heart of gold,
And who but my lady Greensleeves.

She passes in front of the first suitor. Taking his hand and that of the other suitor, she walks round with them in a circle. They also join hands, held high and extended.

The introduction should be played here to allow the actors to turn in place. Greensleeves and the two men face the audience, they gazing at her, with hands on their hearts.

VERSE 4.

Greensleeves, now farewell, adieu,

The suitors take her outstretched hands; all take three steps to R., one to L.

God I pray to prosper thee !
For I am still thy lover true,

They repeat the above dance step twice.

Come once again and love me!

They all take the steps to R. and stop.

Chorus.

For oh, Greensleeves was all my joy,
And oh, Greensleeves was my delight,

They repeat twice the dance step described for verse 4, moving towards stage L.

MY LADY GREENSLEEVES

And oh, Greensleeves was my heart of gold,

The two men release Greensleeves' hands, they take three steps downstage, and turn, facing the lady, barring her way with joined hands.

And who but my lady Greensleeves.

Greensleeves laughs, breaks through their barrier, and runs off L. The suitors watch her despondently.

The introduction is repeated twice, rallentando, to allow the young men to exchange glances, pick up their unwanted presents from the ground, heave a sigh or two, and depart R.

X. *THE GREEN WEDDING*

X. THE GREEN WEDDING

Rather fast

English

1– There was a Squire liv'd in the East, a
Squire of high de - gree, Who went
court - ing of a coun - try girl, a
come - ly maid was she; But
when her fa - ther heard of it, an
an - gry man was he, He re -
quest - ed of his daugh - ter dear to
shun his com - pan - y. *Refrain:* To my
ral - ly, dal - ly, dil - lo, ral - ly, dal - ly, day. To my
ral - ly, dal - ly, dil - lo, ral - ly, dal - ly, day.

X. THE GREEN WEDDING

2. There was a farmer liv'd close by, he had an only son,
   Who came courting of this girl until her love he thought he'd
       won;
   Her mother gave him her consent, her father his likewise,
   Until she cried, "I am undone!" and tears fell from her eyes.
   To my rally, dally, dillo, rally, dally, day.
   To my rally, dally, dillo, rally, dally, day.

3. She wrote the squire a letter and seal'd it with her hand,
   And she said, "This day I'm to be wed unto another man."
   The first few lines he look'd upon he smiled and thus did say,
   "O I may deprive him of his bride all on his wedding day."
   Refrain

4. He wrote her back another, "Go dress yourself in green;
   In a suit all of the same at your wedding I'll be seen;
   In a suit all of the same to your wedding I'll repair,
   O my dearest dear, I'll have you yet in spite of all that's there."
   Refrain

5. He looked East, he lookèd West, he look'd all o'er his land,
   And there came to him full eight score men, all of a Scottish
       band.
   He armèd them with sword and staff, a single man went he,
   Then all the way to the wedding-hall went the company
       dressed in green.
   Refrain

THE GREEN WEDDING

6. When he came to the wedding-hall, they unto him did say:
"You are welcome, Sir, you're welcome, Sir, where have you
spent the day?"
He laughed at them, he scorned at them, and unto them did
say,
"You may have seen my merry men come riding by this way."
Refrain

7. The squire he took a glass of wine and filled it to the brim,
"Here is health unto the man," said he, "the man they call the
groom;
Here's health unto the man," said he, "who may enjoy his bride,
Though another man may love her too, and take her from his
side."
Refrain

8. Then up and spoke the farmer's son, an angry man was he:
"If it is to fight that you come here, 'tis I'm the man for thee!"
"It's not to fight that I am here, but friendship for to show,
So let me kiss your bonny bride, and away from thee I'll go."
Refrain

9. He took her by the waist so small, and by the grass-green
sleeve,
And he led her from the wedding-hall, of no one asking leave.
The band did play, the bugles sound, most glorious to be seen,
And all the way to Headingbourne Town went the company
dressed in green.
Refrain

X. THE GREEN WEDDING

PRESENTATION: A chorus sings while the players pantomime the action. The army calls for "eight score" men, but the requirement need not be taken literally! Any number from eight up makes a convincing array.

STAGING: An outdoor setting is delightful for this ballad. An open clearing among trees is ideal, the only large stage property being a log, downstage left. The small properties necessary are a tray with wine bottle and glasses, a hunting horn, two pieces of writing paper, and a child's ball.

COSTUMING: English costumes of the eighteenth century seem appropriate, though mediaeval attire would be equally picturesque, the merry band being dressed in Robin Hood green.

ACTION: The timing of the action depends upon the conditions of staging, and by careful rehearsal confusion will be eliminated. The marching must be accurately timed and smartly executed. If the performance is given out-of-doors the actors have to approach the scene in full view of the audience before making their official entrance. Again, careful planning is necessary.

VERSE 1.

There was a Squire liv'd in the East, a squire of high degree,
The country girl enters from left, the squire from right; they advance towards each other, taking seven steps. He walks boldly; her manner is modest and gentle.

Who went courting of a country girl, a comely maid was she;
They assume a lover-like attitude, he with his arm round her, she looking up at him smilingly. He caresses her face tenderly on the word "comely."

THE GREEN WEDDING

But when her father heard of it, an angry man was he,
The father stamps angrily in from left, taking seven steps, and parts them rudely on "he."

He requested of his daughter dear to shun his company.
He wags his forefinger admonishingly four times at his daughter, and waves off her suitor with his right hand on the word "shun."

Refrain

The girl walks distractedly around in a circle, mopping her eyes, in rhythm with the music. The squire turns and walks off R., being driven away by the farmer, who follows him threateningly, shaking his fist in rhythm.

VERSE 2.

There was a farmer liv'd close by, he had an only son,
The girl stands weeping, gazing through the woods at her lover's retreating form. From the left the farmer's son enters diffidently, carrying stiffly a posy of wild flowers. He takes seven steps.

Who came courting of this girl until her love he thought he'd won:
On the first syllable of "courting" he drops on both knees, hat in hand, extends his nosegay to her on "girl." She receives it passively on the word "love," and buries her face in it to hide her tears, while he stands hopefully beside her, smiling. The father and mother are seen approaching from opposite directions.

Her mother gave him her consent, her father his likewise,
Her father enters R., her mother L.; the father takes seven steps up to his daughter, the mother an equal number up to the youth. She pats the boy's shoulder approvingly on the second syllable of "consent." The father takes three steps behind his daughter, and

joins the hands of the young pair, on the second syllable of "likewise."

Until she cried, "I am undone!" and tears fell from her eyes.
Snatching her hand away, the girl takes several running steps across to the left, downstage, stopping on "cried" and throwing the nosegay down on the ground. On the second syllable of the word "undone" she glances tragically at the others and then continues to run away from them, downstage left, weeping copiously, and sinks on the log.

Refrain

The mother and father go off, upstage left, reassuring the youth, who walks between them. They beam at him, nodding their heads rhythmically, and patting him on the back. Bewildered at their effusiveness he turns his head alternately right and left, in time with the music. The girl continues to weep, her shoulders heaving rhythmically, during the first line of the refrain; during the second line she wipes her eyes, regaining composure rapidly as an idea strikes her. She pantomimes writing a letter on a piece of paper taken from her pocket.

VERSE 3.

She wrote the squire a letter and seal'd it with her hand,
A little country boy enters from the back centre, tossing a ball in the air. She beckons to him on "wrote," pantomimes sealing the letter and hands it to the child. She indicates where to take it on the word "hand."

And she said, "This day I'm to be wed unto another man."
She turns and walks off upstage left, disconsolately. The boy takes four steps across the stage towards the right, meets the squire

coming in the opposite direction, touches his cap on the second syllable of "unto," and hands the missive to the squire, on the word "man."

The first few lines he look'd upon he smiled and thus did say,
The squire opens the letter hurriedly, reads it and laughs. The child looks on.

"O I may deprive him of his bride all on his wedding day."
Folding his arms, and standing feet apart, the squire nods pensively.

Refrain

He strides up and down the stage impatiently, evidently thinking hard, glancing at the note from time to time. The boy tosses his ball unconcernedly.

Verse 4.

The squire seats himself on the log, downstage left, and pantomimes writing a letter on paper produced from an inner pocket, occasionally pausing to compose his sentences. The child rolls and throws his ball throughout the verse.

Refrain

He beckons to the little boy, twice, indicating the letter in three gestures, during the first line. In line two he produces a coin from his pocket, gives it to the boy and points offstage L. three times, while the child runs out in that direction.

Verse 5.

He lookèd East, he lookèd West, he look'd all o'er his land,
He rises, shades his eyes with his right hand, and gazes off to left and right. He blows his horn vigorously.

THE GREEN WEDDING

And there came to him full eight score men, all of a Scottish band.
He armèd then with sword and staff, a single man went he,

The company come marching in two by two from R., occupying the entire width of the stage. Those in front mark time till all are in, and halt on the final "he." The squire takes three steps to the centre of the stage and stands with his back to the audience, facing his men as if reviewing them, till the end of line three.

Then all the way to the wedding-hall went the company dressed in
*   green.*

The squire takes seven steps directly to the head of the column, while the company salute with their right hands.

Refrain

The entire company, led by the squire, right wheels and marches down and round in a circle, taking up a position in two straight lines on stage R, facing stage L.

VERSE 6.

When he came to the wedding-hall they unto him did say:

The father conducts his daughter, entering from stage L., followed by the mother and the youth. The parson brings up the rear. The girl is dressed in a green gown.

"You are welcome, Sir, you're welcome, Sir, where have you spent
*   the day?"*

The father bustles over to the squire, nodding twice on the "welcomes" and extending his right hand on "have." The girl is in the centre, the mother, the farmer's son, and the parson, are to the left.

He laughed at them, he scorned at them, and unto them did say,

Ignoring the outstretched hand the squire laughs, and snaps his fingers.

THE GREEN WEDDING

"You may have seen my merry men come riding by this way."
Jerking his head in the direction of his company, he strides about
in their vicinity. The girl looks at him with admiration; the father,
abashed by the refusal of his overtures, regards the squire sus-
piciously. The mother attempts to spruce up the bridegroom by
smoothing his clothes. The parson looks slightly bewildered, and
peers short-sightedly from side to side.

Refrain

The company turns left, and right wheels, marching across the
back of the stage, as in verse five, marking time. They face front
and halt on the last three beats of the music. Throughout the refrain
the squire stands with folded arms, facing front. With hands
clasped behind him the father strides nervously back and forth
downstage. The farmer's son makes appealing gestures to the girl,
who turns her head from him. They repeat these movements rhythmically to the end of the refrain. The mother, sensing the situation,
clasps her hands and sways from side to side. The parson makes
for the log, sits down, gets out his prayer book and starts to read
(rhythmically!). On the second line of the refrain the little boy
enters from upstage L., carrying a tray on which are a wine bottle
and glasses. He stands near the squire.

VERSE 7.

The squire he took a glass of wine and filled it to the brim,
The squire jauntily takes the bottle in one hand, a glass in the other,
and pantomimes pouring out a drink. The others gaze at him, aghast
at his temerity, standing still till the end of the verse.

"Here is health unto the man," said he, "the man they call the groom;
Here's health unto the man," said he, "who may enjoy his bride,
Though another man may love her too, and take her from his side."

THE GREEN WEDDING

With a flourish of his arm he indicates the farmer's son (who stands looking oafish), bowing to him ironically and pledging his health.

Refrain

The soldiers mark time, halting at the end of the music; the mother crosses to her daughter and fusses over her, patting her hand rhythmically. The father goes to the farmer's son and tries to improve his morale by gesticulations of encouragement. The squire walks up and down reviewing his company, finishing in the centre of the stage.

VERSE 8.

Then up and spoke the farmer's son, an angry man was he:
The groom, brushing aside the father, takes five strides over to the squire.

"If it is to fight that you come here, 'tis I'm the man for thee!"
He squares his shoulders, and clenches his fists, frowning at his rival.

"It's not to fight that I am here, but friendship for to show,
The squire claps him on the shoulder suavely.

So let me kiss your bonny bride, and away from thee I'll go."
The squire strides over to the girl in three steps and kisses her on "away." Everyone else shows great interest.

Refrain

The soldiers mark time, halting at the end of the music; the father, impatient of delay, beckons to the parson, at the same time taking four steps over to the groom. The parson walks four steps upstage, and turns facing the audience. The groom, led by the father, takes

THE GREEN WEDDING

four steps downstage, turns, faces the parson and kneels. The preceding action occupies line 1. During line 2. the father moves one or two paces to the right, and turns, facing the groom. The mother escorts her daughter over to the parson and leaves her on the right of the groom where she kneels, and herself takes up a position on the right of the wedding group, as the music ends. The squire walks along the ranks, appearing to give instructions to his men.

VERSE 9.

The soldiers turn right, the foremost half of the company marches two steps, leaving a space in the middle of the column. They all mark time for a line and a half. The squire takes four strides over to the girl, snatches her by the waist, and starts with her towards the middle of the company. By the word "wedding hall" they have reached the protecting ranks, and wheeling left they all march round the stage until the end of the verse. The other members of the group: father, mother, parson, and the groom (who rises from his feet), show great consternation and anger, and yet are powerless to act. They huddle together in the centre of the stage, arguing violently. The little boy marches importantly behind the soldiers.

Refrain

The column files out, R. The wedding group **go** home L. in great dismay, during the second line of the music.

XI. *THE LAIRD O' COCKPEN*

XI. THE LAIRD O' COCKPEN

Scottish

Lady Carolina Nairne

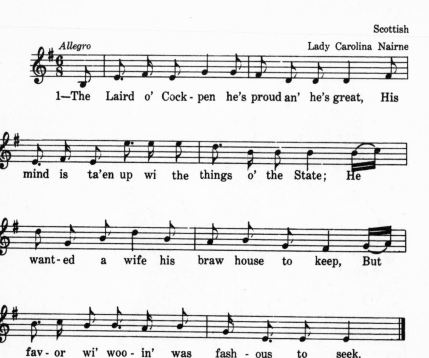

1—The Laird o' Cock-pen he's proud an' he's great, His mind is ta'en up wi the things o' the State; He want-ed a wife his braw house to keep, But fav-or wi' woo-in' was fash-ous to seek.

XI. THE LAIRD O' COCKPEN

2. Doun by the dyke-side a lady did dwell,
   At his table-head he thocht she'd look well:
   M'Cleish's ae dochter o' Claversha' Lee,
   A pennyless lass, wi' a lang pedigree.

3. His wig was weel-pouthered, as gude as when new,
   His waistcoat was white, his coat it was blue;
   He put on a ring, a sword, and cock'd hat;
   And wha could refuse the Laird wi' a' that?

4. He mounted his mare and he rade cannilie;
   An' rapped at the yett o' Claversha' Lee.
   "Gae tell Mistress Jean to come speedily ben;
   She's wanted to speak wi' the Laird o' Cockpen."

5. Mistress Jean she was makin' the elder-flower wine —
   "What the deil brings the Laird here at sic a like time?"
   She put aff her apron, an' on her silk goun,
   Her mutch wi' red ribbons, an' gaed awa' doun.

6. An' when she came ben, he bobbit fu' low;
   An' what was his errand he soon let her know.
   Amazed was the Laird when the lady said —"Na,"
   An' wi' a laigh curtsie she turnèd awa'.

7. Dumbfounder'd was he — but nae sigh did he gi'e;
   He mounted his mare and he rade cannilie;
   An' aften he thocht, as he gaed through the glen,
   "She was daft to refuse the Laird o' Cockpen."

8. And now that the Laird his exit had made,
   Mistress Jean she reflected on what she had said;
   "Oh! for ane I'll get better, it's waur I'll get ten—
   I was daft to refuse the Laird o' Cockpen."

111

XI. THE LAIRD O' COCKPEN

PRESENTATION: The comic element in this ballad can be heightened by an interpretation of the narrative in silent pantomime, accompanied by choral singing, the dialogue being spoken or sung by the actors. If it seems preferable, the narrative could also be read throughout in Scottish dialect.

STAGING: Stage L. represents the Laird's domain; stage R. is the home of Mistress Jean. She has a bench or chair on which to sit. There is also a table R.; a bowl is placed on it in verse 3.

COSTUMING: The Laird's outfit is in accordance with the description in verse 3. Mistress Jean's clothes are suggested in verse 5. The servant girl wears a dress, with a full skirt, an apron, and a mob cap. (The Laird actually lived in the eighteenth century.)

ACTION: The facial expressions must be exaggerated, the gestures emphatic, as little physical movement occurs in this ballad.

VERSE 1. If the stage boasts a front curtain, Mistress Jean may be discovered, as it parts, seated on a bench, sewing. If there is no curtain she simply walks on R. to the beat of the music, as the Laird struts in from L. Mistress Jean keeps on sewing throughout the verse. Her maid bustles about the room, sweeping and dusting it — rhythmically ! The Laird walks up and down on stage L. for fifteen steps. He demonstrates his pride, his interest in state affairs, his desire for a wife, and his irritation at the thought of bothering to go a-wooing. Facial expression is very important here.

VERSE 2.
> *Doun by the dyke-side a lady did dwell,*

The Laird points towards Mistress Jean's home, and shows animation.

> *At his table-head he thocht she'd look well:*

He nods his head complacently four times. Mistress Jean and the servant continue in lines 1–2 with their actions as in verse 1.

THE LAIRD O' COCKPEN

M'Cleish's ae dochter o' Claversha' Lee

He wags his forefinger four times in Mistress Jean's direction. Jean rises, curtsies, and smiles at the audience.

A pennyless lass, wi' a lang pedigree.

The Laird, Jean, and the maid, pantomime turning out their pockets, then measure imaginary pedigrees with their arms, using large gestures.

VERSE 3.

His wig was weel-pouthered, as gude as when new,

The Laird points to his wig, and preens himself. The servant goes off R. taking eight steps, using lines 1–2 of the verse in which to do so. Mistress Jean sits down and resumes her sewing.

His waistcoat was white, his coat it was blue;

The Laird shows his waistcoat and his coat to the audience. Mistress Jean continues to sew.

He put on a ring, a sword, and cock'd hat;

The Laird pantomimes putting on a ring and a sword. He dons his cocked hat which he has been carrying in his hand. The servant enters from R. with a bowl, which she places on the table.

And wha could refuse the Laird wi' a' that?

The Laird strikes an attitude, his face reflecting complete self-satisfaction. Mistress Jean begins to stir the wine. The maid stands on her left, watching operations.

VERSE 4.

He mounted his mare and he rade cannilie;

The Laird strides an imaginary horse and "trots" toward the centre of the stage, facing Jean's abode. She is still stirring the wine. The servant assists her.

THE LAIRD O' COCKPEN

An' rapped at the yett o' Claversha' Lee.

The Laird knocks four times on the imaginary door. The servant takes three steps towards him, halting at the "door." Mistress Jean stops her task and listens intently.

> *"Gae tell Mistress Jean to come speedily ben;*
> *She's wanted to speak wi' the Laird o' Cockpen."*

The Laird speaks the lines very haughtily to the servant, who drops a curtsy, and looks very much overawed.

VERSE 5.

Mistress Jean she was makin' the elder-flower wine

The Laird steps into the house. Mistress Jean stirs the wine with assumed interest. The servant takes three steps and halts beside her mistress, drawing her attention to the important visitor.

"What the deil brings the Laird at sic a like time?"

Mistress Jean utters the line with real or affected astonishment. The Laird waits impatiently. The servant stands still, goggle-eyed.

She put aff her apron, an' on her silk goun,

Mistress Jean removes her apron, and pantomimes arraying herself in a silk gown. The maid helps her. The Laird waits until the end of the verse, getting more and more impatient.

Her mutch wi' red ribbons, an' gaed awa' doun.

Mistress Jean pantomimes putting on her mutch, and crosses to the Laird. The servant stands still, watching expectantly.

VERSE 6.

An' when she came ben, he bobbit fu' low;

The Laird bows, Mistress Jean curtsies.

An' what was his errand he soon let her know.

The Laird puts his lace handkerchief on the floor, kneels upon it, placing his hand on his heart. Mistress Jean watches him, motionless.

THE LAIRD O' COCKPEN

Amazed was the Laird when the lady said —"Na,"
Mistress Jean surveys him with disdain, saying "Na" very loudly
and with great finality. The Laird is too much astonished to move.
The servant raises her hands in amazement and horror.

An' wi' a laigh curtsie she turnèd awa'.
Mistress Jean curtsies ironically, and turns her back. The Laird
rises, discomfited, and picks up his kerchief angrily. The maid's
eyes pop!

VERSE 7.
Dumfounder'd was he — but nae sigh did he gi'e;
The Laird struggles to overcome his feelings. They all stand still.

He mounted his mare and he rade cannilie;
An' aften he thocht, as he gaed through the glen,
"She was daft to refuse the Laird o' Cockpen."
The Laird "mounts" and "rides" round in a circle, stage L., saying
line 4 to the audience before he disappears L. The maid watches
Mistress Jean, who holds the same position, in the centre of the
stage.

VERSE 8.
And now that the Laird his exit had made,
Mistress Jean takes three involuntary steps after the Laird. The
maid takes three steps after her mistress. Both follow him with
their eyes.

Mistress Jean she reflected on what she had said;
Mistress Jean faces the audience, looking thoughtful. The servant
eyes her with misgivings.

"Oh! for ane I'll get better, it's waur I'll get ten —
Mistress Jean says the line regretfully to the audience. The maid
nods four times.

THE LAIRD O' COCKPEN

I was daft to refuse the Laird o' Cockpen."

Mistress Jean says the line remorsefully, stamps her foot on the word "daft," and runs off R. at the end of the line. The maid watches her, and as she disappears may form an echo, as she confides in the audience, "She was daft to refuse the Laird o' Cockpen," before running out after her mistress.

XII. *THE OLD WOMAN & THE PEDLAR*

XII. THE OLD WOMAN
AND THE PEDLAR

Not too fast

English

1— There was an old wo-man, as I've heard tell,

Fal, lal, lal lal lal lal la,

She went to mar-ket her eggs for to sell,

Fal, lal, lal lal lal lal la,

She went to mar-ket as I've heard say,

Fal, lal, lal lal lal lal la,

She fell a-sleep on the King's high-way,

Fal, lal, lal lal lal lal la,

XII. THE OLD WOMAN & THE PEDLAR

2. There came by a pedlar whose name was Stout,
   Fal, lal, lal lal lal lal la,
   He cut her petticoats round about,
   Fal, lal, lal lal lal lal la,
   He cut her petticoats up to her knees,
   Fal, lal, lal lal lal lal la,
   Which made the old woman to shiver and sneeze.
   Fal, lal, lal lal lal lal la,

3. When this little woman did first awake,
   Fal, lal, lal lal lal lal la,
   She began to shiver and began to shake;
   Fal, lal, lal lal lal lal la,
   She began to wonder, she began to cry,
   Fal, lal, lal lal lal lal la,
   "Oh! deary me, this can never be I!"
   Fal, lal, lal lal lal lal la,

4. "But if it be I, as I hope it be,
   Fal, lal, lal lal lal lal la,
   I've a dog at home that I'm sure knows me.
   Fal, lal, lal lal lal lal la,
   If it be I, he will wag his tail,
   Fal, lal, lal lal lal lal la,
   And if it's not I, he will bark and wail."
   Fal, lal, lal lal lal lal la,

5. Home went the old woman all in the dark,
   Fal, lal, lal lal lal lal la,
   Then up got her dog and began to bark.
   Fal, lal, lal lal lal lal la,
   He began to bark; she began to cry,
   Fal, lal, lal lal lal lal la,
   "Deary me, dear! this is none of I!"
   Fal, lal, lal lal lal lal la,

XII. THE OLD WOMAN & THE PEDLAR

PRESENTATION: The music is so gay that one of the most successful methods of presenting this ballad is with choral accompaniment. The chorus has plenty of opportunity to participate in the creation of atmosphere; they must sing the "fal, lal's" trippingly, and the dialogue lines emphatically, in a slightly slower tempo. They may dramatise with their voices such lines as, "She began to shiver and began to shake"; after the words "shiver and sneeze" they may give one huge concerted sneeze, and after "bark and wail" a realistic canine howl affords great amusement. Another effective way of presenting the ballad is to have the old woman sing or say her lines of dialogue, while the "dog" does his own barking.

STAGING: One side of the stage represents the old woman's house, the other side is the highroad. A sign, on which are painted the words, "King's Highway" is sufficient indication of the locality.

COSTUMING: The old woman must have a voluminous skirt, made of colored paper to facilitate its being cut by the pedlar. Underneath the skirt she should wear a pair of old-fashioned bloomers which reach below the knees. Her garb also includes a shawl, a blouse, and a mob cap; she carries a market-basket. The pedlar looks very jaunty, in spite of his ragged attire, which is modelled on the familiar pattern for young men found in the Mother Goose rhymes. He carries a sack from which he takes a large pair of scissors during verse 2. The dog's head is easily made from paper, while blankets may be used to camouflage the rest of the actor's body. The more mongrel the animal, the more amusing the effect!

ACTION: Great variety is possible in the interpretation of the three rôles in this ballad. The dog's antics, the old woman's dismay, and the pedlar's devilment, may be portrayed in many ways, always, however, with strict regard for the definite rhythm of the music.

THE OLD WOMAN & THE PEDLAR

VERSE 1. To introductory bars of music (the chorus sing a few fal, lal's for this), enter from R. the old woman, followed by her dog on all fours.

> *There was an old woman as I've heard tell,*

The dog runs to his "kennel" upstage R., lying down on the word "tell"; the old woman takes three steps in his direction.

> *Fal, lal etc.*

The old woman shakes her finger at him four times, warning him not to leave home while she is gone. The dog listens but does not move.

> *She went to market her eggs for to sell,*
> *Fal, lal etc.*
> *She went to market as I've heard say,*
> *Fal, lal etc.*

The dog lies quietly, as in line 2. The old woman trudges round the stage, carrying her basket; she takes a circular route for fifteen steps, getting more and more tired as she walks; she lays down her basket at the end of line 6.

> *She fell asleep on the King's highway,*
> *Fal, lal etc.*

She yawns, rubs her eyes, lies down and goes to sleep.

VERSE 2.

> *There came by a pedlar whose name was Stout,*
> *Fal, lal etc.*

Enter from L. the pedlar, skipping lightheartedly for three steps. He stops abruptly, seeing the old woman, conceives his mischievous idea, and dives into his sack for the scissors, which he flourishes in the air.

THE OLD WOMAN & THE PEDLAR

He cut her petticoats round about,
Fal, lal etc.
He cut her petticoats up to her knees,
Fal, lal etc.
Which made the old woman to shiver and sneeze.

The pedlar cuts off the old woman's skirt, using his scissors recklessly, with enormous gestures, grinning the while at the audience; he rolls the old woman over in order to complete his job thoroughly. During line 7 she pantomimes shivering violently.

Fal, lal etc.

She continues to shiver. The pedlar skips off R., laughing to himself.

VERSE 3.

When this little woman did first awake,
Fal, lal etc.

The old woman sits up, rubs her eyes, and stares around in a dazed fashion.

She began to shiver and began to shake;

She shivers and shakes.

Fal, lal etc.

She rises to her feet.

She began to wonder, she began to cry,
Fal, lal etc.

She looks down at her shorn petticoat, showing great dismay and horror.

"Oh! deary me, this can never be I!"
Fal, lal etc.

She turns round and round, looking down at her petticoat, twisting to view it from every angle. Finally she faces the audience, pantomiming her complete bewilderment.

THE OLD WOMAN & THE PEDLAR

> *"But if it be I, as I hope it be,*
> *Fal, lal etc.*

She looks at the audience, points to herself, and looks hopeful, nodding her head wisely.

> *I've a dog at home that I'm sure knows me.*

She points to the dog, who is still lying "at home."

> *Fal, lal etc.*

She skips round, pleased to have a solution to her problem.

> *If it be I, he will wag his tail,*
> *Fal, lal etc.*

She points to herself and "wags her tail," skipping round on the "fal, lal's."

> *And if it's not I, he will bark and wail,*
> *Fal, lal etc.*

She looks mournfully at the audience, shaking her head, while the chorus imitates the dog's howls. On the "fal lal's" the old woman hops round rather sadly, picking up her basket as the music ends.

VERSE 5.

> *Home went the old woman all in the dark,*
> *Fal, lal etc.*

The old woman trudges "home," taking seven steps to get there.

> *Then up got her dog and began to bark.*

She looks down at her dog; the dog jumps up and down four times, showing great agitation. His leaps and bounds are faultlessly rhythmic.

> *Fal, lal etc.*

He takes four leaps towards her, as she retreats in fear.

He began to bark, she began to cry,
Fal, lal etc.

The dog leaps round her, taking eight bounds. She stands crying.

"Deary me, dear! this is none of I!"

She shakes her head and laments to the audience. The dog continues to show great agitation.

Fal, lal etc.

She goes off L., followed by her dog, still jumping excitedly. If, by the end of verse 5 the players are not yet offstage, the chorus may hum the last line or two of the music, so that the scene ends neatly.

XIII. *O SOLDIER, SOLDIER*

XIII. O SOLDIER, SOLDIER,

Appalachian

Allegro

1—"O sol - dier, sol - dier, won't you mar - ry me With your mus - ket, fife and drum? "Oh, no, sweet maid, I can-not mar - ry thee, For I have no coat to put on." Then up she went to her grand - fa - ther's chest, And got him a coat of the ve - ry, ve - ry best, She got him a coat of the ve - ry, ve - ry best, And the sol - dier put it on.

Fine.

D.C.

XIII. O SOLDIER, SOLDIER

2. "O soldier, soldier, won't you marry me
    With your musket, fife and drum?"
   "Oh, no, sweet maid, I cannot marry thee,
    For I have no hat to put on."
    Then up she went to her grandfather's chest,
    And got him a hat of the very, very best,
    She got him a hat of the very, very best,
    And the soldier put it on.

3. "O soldier, soldier, won't you marry me
    With your musket, fife and drum?"
   "Oh, no, sweet maid, I cannot marry thee,
    For I have no gloves to put on."
    Then up she went to her grandfather's chest,
    And got him some gloves of the very, very best,
    She got him some gloves of the very, very best,
    And the soldier put them on.

4. "O soldier, soldier, won't you marry me
    With your musket, fife and drum?"
   "Oh, no, sweet maid, I cannot marry thee,
    For I have no boots to put on."
    Then up she went to her grandfather's chest,
    And got him some boots of the very, very best,
    She got him some boots of the very, very best,
    And the soldier put them on.

5. "O soldier, soldier, won't you marry me
    With your musket, fife and drum?"
   "Oh, no, sweet maid, I cannot marry thee,
    For I have a wife of my own."

XIII. O SOLDIER, SOLDIER

PRESENTATION: Silent pantomime with choral accompaniment is very effective for this song, though it is also charming when the dialogue is sung by the actors, and the narrative parts only by the choir. The former method is described here.

STAGING: The only property is a large old-fashioned chest, containing coat, hat, gloves, and boots. It is placed on stage L.

COSTUMING: Although this song is of English origin it seems to be little known in the Old Country, and yet it is very generally remembered here especially in the ·Eastern mountain regions. Costumes of the Revolutionary period are appropriate, and the various articles specified in the song must be provided. The soldier is clad in shirt and trousers when he makes his appearance; the girl is simply but attractively attired.

ACTION: INTRODUCTION. The last eight measures of the music are played on a ·trumpet or other brass instrument. If none is available try to get a military effect on the piano! The soldier marches haughtily from stage R., followed by the girl, pleading with him. Each takes fifteen steps across and round the stage in a circle, finishing on stage R. as the music ceases.

VERSE 1.

  "O soldier, soldier, won't you marry me
The girl entreats; the soldier takes no notice.

  With your musket, fife and drum?"
The girl pantomimes shouldering a musket, playing on a fife, and beating a drum.

  "Oh, no, sweet maid, I cannot marry thee,
The soldier shakes his head; the girl looks sorrowful.

O SOLDIER, SOLDIER

For I have no coat to put on."

The soldier thinks quickly of an excuse, then indicates that he lacks a coat. (The chorus makes a perceptible hesitation between the words "no" and "coat" and repeats this pause at the same place in the other verses.)

Then up she went to her grandfather's chest,

The girl takes seven running steps over to the chest, lifts out the coat. The soldier stands quite still, looking annoyed and embarrassed.

And she got him a coat of the very, very best,

The girl holds up the coat, admiring it.

She got him a coat of the very, very best,

She runs back with it to the soldier, who is still uncompromising.

And the soldier put it on.

He reluctantly puts on the coat, with her assistance.

Note

Interlude: In order to give movement and variety the four measures beginning, "Oh, no, sweet maid" may be played or hummed between the verses. Here the soldier moves impatiently to the centre, upstage, followed by the girl. Seven steps.

Verse 2.

Same as verse 1. with *Hat* as focus of attention.
Interlude: The soldier moves downstage centre, followed by the persistent maiden.

Verse 3.

Same as verse 1. with *Gloves* as focus of attention.
Interlude: The soldier walks over to stage R. in a vain attempt to escape. The girl trails after him.

O SOLDIER, SOLDIER

VERSE 4.

Same as verse 1. with *Boots* as focus of attention.
Interlude: The girl takes the unwilling soldier's arm, leaning upon him lovingly, as they walk across to stage L.

VERSE 5.

> *"O soldier, soldier, won't you marry me*
> *With your musket, fife· and drum?"*
> *"Oh, no, sweet maid, I cannot marry thee,*

Same as verse 1, lines 1–3.

> *For I have a wife of my own!"*

The soldier sings this line loudly, hoarsely, and desperately! (whether the other "dialogue" has been sung by the players or not.) The girl falls in a faint.

CURTAIN

(If there is no curtain, the soldier must, after a short pause, help the girl to her feet and they both take a bow.)

XIV. *THE PEDLAR*

XIV. THE PEDLAR

Smoothly

Russian

1——Ah, my heav - y pack is near - ly bursting With
silk and lace and jew - els rare, And the
weight on my wear - y should - ers
Al - most more than I can bear,
And the weight on my wear - y should - ers
Al - most more than I can bear,
Chorus: Hai - da, hai - da, hai - da, hai - da,
hai - da, hai - da, hai - da, da.
Hai - da, hai - da, hai - da, hai - da,
Al - most more than I can bear.

XIV. THE PEDLAR

2. "Little maiden, will you buy a jewel
   From all the pretty things I bring?"
   "Oh, such lovely wares, kind pedlar,
   Will two pennies buy a ring?
   Oh, such lovely wares, kind pedlar,
   Will two pennies buy a ring?"
   Haida, etc.

3. "I'll not take your pennies, gentle maiden,
   Nay, 'twould be a trade unfair,
   For your joy's a gem more priceless
   Than are all my jewels rare.
   For your joy's a gem more priceless
   Than are all my jewels rare."
   Haida, etc.

4. "Ah, my burden light has grown as laughter
   As toward the setting sun I start,
   Now has gone the weight from my shoulders,
   There's a singing in my heart.
   Now has gone the weight from my shoulders,
   There's a singing in my heart."
   Haida, etc.

XIV. THE PEDLAR

PRESENTATION: This Russian ballad has a subtlety and a wistful charm not often met with in English folklore; the melody is a most beautiful example of folk music, and it is very well known in its many variants. The music lends the action much of its character, so that silent pantomime, with choral accompaniment, seems the most fitting method of interpretation. Indeed, in this particular example, the whole presentation would be marred by a mere recitation of the lines; it is *made* by the charm of the music.

STAGING: An outdoor setting is delightful, the pedlar wending his way through trees, or across a meadow, towards the little maiden. An indoor setting has also many possibilities: the pedlar may approach the stage from the auditorium, mounting the platform by means of steps.

COSTUMING: The maiden wears a brightly colored Russian peasant costume, with a scarf on her head, tied under the chin. The pedlar wears a smock, baggy trousers, and high boots. On his back he carries a pack containing jewelry, gay scarves, and laces.

ACTION: As there is not much physical movement, the gestures must be particularly well-defined, and the changes of mood very clearly indicated by facial expression. Because of the slightness of the plot extra care should be taken with the details of costuming and setting.

Verse 1.

The pedlar, carrying his pack, approaches the stage, either from the back of the auditorium, up a flight of steps, and on to the platform, or simply from stage L., in which case he walks wearily round the stage, as if on a long journey. He takes twenty four steps.

Chorus. The pedlar continues on his way for seven steps, laying down his pack in the centre of the stage on the eighth bar. The peas-

THE PEDLAR

ant girl dances in from R., also taking seven steps. Hers, however, are gay and carefree, in contrast to those of the pedlar. During the next eight measures the pedlar begins to open his pack in a listless fashion, kneeling and facing the audience. The girl dances round him meanwhile, in an ever-narrowing circle, as her curiosity gets the better of her.

VERSE 2.

> *"Little maiden, will you buy a jewel*
> *From all the pretty things I bring?"*

The pedlar holds up some jewelry to the little maiden who stands enraptured at the sight of his wares. She rises on tiptoe, clasping her hands together.

> *"Oh, such lovely wares, kind pedlar,*
> *Will two pennies buy a ring?*

She reaches down, and holds at arm's length some of the contents of his pack, admiring them with great enthusiasm; she pulls two pennies from her pocket, offering them to the pedlar, who watches her benevolently.

> *Oh, such lovely wares, kind pedlar,*
> *Will two pennies buy a ring?"*

She dances round the pedlar's pack, and again offers him her money.

Chorus. The pedlar takes all sorts of finery from his store, holding them out for her inspection; the girl dances round him and his pack, fascinatedly. She again proffers him her pennies on the last four measures.

VERSE 3.

> *"I'll not take your pennies, gentle maiden,*
> *Nay, 'twould be a trade unfair,*

The pedlar stands up, gives her a ring, and with a gesture, refuses the money held out to him. She looks surprised, then delighted.

135

THE PEDLAR

> *For your joy's a gem more priceless*
> *Than are all my jewels rare.*

She puts the ring on her finger, gazing at it with joy. The pedlar looks contentedly at her, and then at his wares.

> *For your joy's a gem more priceless*
> *Than are all my jewels rare."*

She throws him a kiss and dances off R., still admiring her new possession; the pedlar watches her happily.

Chorus. The pedlar cheerfully re-assembles all his goods, restoring them to his pack, which he closes as the chorus ends.

VERSE 4.

> *"Ah, my burden light has grown as laughter*

The pedlar lifts his pack and slings it without effort on to his back.

> *As toward the setting sun I start,*

He turns towards the right, gazing into the distance with radiantly happy face.

> *Now has gone the weight from my shoulders,*
> *There's a singing in my heart.*
> *Now has gone, etc.*

If the performance is taking place outdoors, the pedlar continues on his way, walking with a sprightly step, disappearing as mysteriously as he came, while the chorus sings lines 3–6 and the refrain. If the setting is a stage, the pedlar walks off R., during lines 3–4. The curtain falls as the chorus sings lines 5–6. There is no need for the final refrain, but it may be sung if desired.

XV. *THE PRETTY DRUMMER*

XV. THE PRETTY DRUMMER

Adapted from the French

Briskly

1- Home from the wars three drum - mers were re -
turn - ing, Home from the wars three
drum - mers were re - turn - - - - ing, Rum, tum,
tum - ti - ti tum, three drum - mers were re - turn - - - ing.

XV. THE PRETTY DRUMMER

2. Each drummer boy had in his mouth a rosebud.
   Each drummer boy had in his mouth a rosebud.
   Rum, tum, tum-ti-ti-tum, had in his mouth a rosebud.

3. High in the tower sat the princess at her window.
   High in the tower sat the princess at her window.
   Rum, tum, tum-ti-ti-tum, the princess at her window.

4. "Pray, drummer fair, give me your pretty rosebud.
   Pray, drummer fair, give me your pretty rosebud.
   Rum, tum, tum-ti-ti-tum, give me your pretty rosebud!"

5. "Give me your heart in turn for it, King's daughter.
   Give me your heart in turn for it, King's daughter.
   Rum, tum, tum-ti-ti-tum, in turn for it, King's daughter."

6. "O drummer boy, go ask it of my father.
   O drummer boy, go ask it of my father.
   Rum, tum, tum-ti-ti-tum, go ask it of my father."

7. "My lord and king, pray may I wed your daughter?
   My lord and king, pray may I wed your daughter?
   Rum, tum, tum-ti-ti-tum, pray may I wed your daughter?"

139

THE PRETTY DRUMMER

8. "O drummer boy, first tell to me your fortune.
   O drummer boy, first tell to me your fortune.
   Rum, tum, tum-ti-ti-tum, first tell to me your fortune."

9. "My lord and king, my drumsticks are my fortune.
   My lord and king, my drumsticks are my fortune.
   Rum, tum, tum-ti-ti-tum, my drumsticks are my fortune."

10. "O drummer boy, your fortune is too scanty.
    O drummer boy, your fortune is too scanty.
    Rum, tum, tum-ti-ti-tum, your fortune is too scanty."

11. "My lord and king, I've ships and gold a-plenty.
    My lord and king, I've ships and gold a-plenty.
    Rum, tum, tum-ti-ti-tum, I've ships and gold a-plenty."

12. "O drummer boy, then you may wed my daughter.
    O drummer boy, then you may wed my daughter.
    Rum, tum, tum-ti-ti-tum, then you may wed my daughter."

13. "My lord and king, I will not wed your daughter.
    My lord and king, I will not wed your daughter.
    Rum, tum, tum-ti-ti-tum, I will not wed your daughter."

14. "In my own land we have far fairer maidens.
    In my own land we have far fairer maidens.
    Rum, tum, tum-ti-ti-tum, we have far fairer maidens!"

XV. THE PRETTY DRUMMER

PRESENTATION: The music for this ballad is delightfully gay so that choral singing is a charming accompaniment to the entire action, which may be carried out in silent pantomime. The dialogue, however may be spoken or sung by the actors themselves. If a chorus is used throughout, the singers may be divided into groups for singing the dialogue lines to avoid monotony in a song of so many verses; or, if good soloists are available, they may do this; the full choir carrying the purely narrative parts.

STAGING: This may be elaborate, or very simple, according to the circumstances of production. Mediaeval-looking wall hangings may be introduced effectively; a fleur-de-lys pattern is a typical one. During the first five verses the princess must be high above the level of the stage; she could stand on a stool behind a screen. No other furniture is necessary.

COSTUMING: The drummers wear bright jerkins, with tights, or long stockings; they should have jaunty little caps on their heads and carry drums and drumsticks. (The drums are easily made from large ice-cream containers, or from other large round boxes. They should be beaten only in pantomime.) The princess wears a flowing mediaeval gown and a mediaeval head-dress. She carries a chiffon handkerchief. The king wears a very conventional royal robe and should be well padded to look sufficiently pompous in his role of "heavy father." He has, of course, a crown, perhaps, even a sceptre.

ACTION: The entry of the drummer boys can be made truly military if the introductory bars are played on a bugle or some other brass instrument. If not, the piano will do!

VERSE 1. The princess sits throughout the verse in her tower, stage L., waving her handkerchief in rhythm with the music.

Home from the wars three drummers were returning,
The three drummers enter R. in single file, the principal drummer

THE PRETTY DRUMMER

in the centre. They march briskly to the centre of the stage, in seven steps, facing upstage on the last note of the line. They go through the movements of beating their drums as they march, and carry rosebuds in their mouths.

Home from the wars three drummers were returning.
The drummers take eight marching steps abreast upstage.

Rum, tum, tum-ti-ti-tum, three drummers were returning.
They turn in place (aways rightabout), facing downstage on the last note of the line. Their movements must be precise and in strict unison.

VERSE 2.

Each drummer boy had in his mouth a rosebud,
The drummers take seven marching steps downstage, making an about turn on the last note of the line.

Each drummer boy had in his mouth a rosebud,
They march upstage seven steps, making an about turn on the last note of the line.

Rum, tum, tum-ti-ti- tum, had in his mouth a rosebud.
They take four steps downstage, then turn in place, facing R. The princess waves to them throughout the verse.

VERSE 3.

High in the tower sat the princess at her window,
High in the tower sat the princess at her window,
The drummer boys, in single file, march round in a circle, then, standing abreast, face the princess. They wave their drumsticks as they march.

Rum, tum, tum-ti-ti- tum, the princess at her window.
They turn in place, beating their drums, and face the princess, who has continued to wave and smile at them.

VERSE 4.

"Pray drummer fair, give me your pretty rosebud,

THE PRETTY DRUMMER

Pray drummer fair, give me your pretty rosebud,
The princess beckons to the central drummer, pointing to his rosebud. He looks surprised, compares notes with his companions, and advances towards the princess, taking the centre of the stage. The other two drummers, in order not to block the main action, in which they are really colorful background, take four slip-steps away from the centre, on the first line, and mark time during the second line.

Rum, tum, tum-ti-ti-tum, give me your pretty rosebud!"
The three drummers turn in place, beating their drums.

VERSE 5.
"Give me your heart, in turn for it, King's daughter,
The Pretty Drummer kneels, asking for the princess' heart. She looks coy, hiding behind her handkerchief. The other two drummers discreetly turn about, taking seven steps downstage, facing each other on the last note of the line.

Give me your heart in turn for it, King's daughter,
The action is the same for the Pretty Drummer and the princess. The other drummers take eight steps forward, changing places.

Rum, tum, tum-ti-ti-tum, in turn for it King's daughter."
The three drummers turn in place, then all face the princess.

VERSE 6.
"O drummer boy, go ask it of my father,
The Pretty Drummer assists the princess to descend from her tower, as she motions towards stage R., indicating her father's presence. The other drummers take eight steps upstage.

O drummer boy, go ask it of my father,
The princess again motions towards stage R. The Pretty Drummer's two companions change places, marching gaily.

Rum, tum, tum-ti-ti-tum, go ask it of my father."
Enter the King from stage R. All the drummers turn in place; the princess does a lively little dance step, turning in place also.

143

THE PRETTY DRUMMER

"My lord and king, pray may I wed your daughter?
My lord and king, pray may I wed your daughter?

The Pretty Drummer bows to the king, indicating the daughter, who watches eagerly. Repeat. The other drummers mark time, watching with interest.

Rum, tum, tum-ti-ti-tum, pray may I wed your daughter?"

The three drummers turn in place; the princess, and even the king, who performs with fitting dignity, do a little dance step.

Verse 8.

"O drummer boy, first tell to me your fortune,
O drummer boy, first tell to me your fortune,

The king pantomimes rubbing coins between finger and thumb; the Pretty Drummer and the princess look downcast. The other two drummers take seven steps downstage, exchanging knowing glances; they turn about and march back to their original positions.

Rum, tum, tum-ti-ti-tum, first tell to me your fortune."

All do their characteristic steps.

Verse 9.

"My lord and king, my drumsticks are my fortune,
My lord and king, my drumsticks are my fortune,

The Pretty Drummer bows low, glances mischievously at his friends, then extends his drumsticks to the king, who turns away in contempt. Repeat. The princess looks apprehensive. The other two drummers mark time, and extend their drumsticks simultaneously with the Pretty Drummer.

Rum, tum, tum-ti-ti-tum, my drumsticks are my fortune."

The king stands frowning; the Pretty Drummer turns in place, extending his drumsticks with exaggerated eagerness. The princess does her little dance step, but sadly. The other two drummers turn in place.

THE PRETTY DRUMMER

"O drummer boy, your fortune is too scanty,
O drummer boy, your fortune is too scanty,

The king pantomimes extreme contempt, the Pretty Drummer looks downcast, so does the princess. The other drummers mark time, awaiting events. Repeat.

Rum tum, tum-ti-ti-tum, your fortune is too scanty."

The king surveys the Pretty Drummer with distaste; the latter turns in place, apparently in great dejection; the princess applies her handkerchief to her eyes; the other drummers turn in place.

VERSE 11.

"My lord and king, I've ships and gold a-plenty,
My lord and king, I've ships and gold a-plenty,

The Pretty Drummer suddenly assumes a jaunty manner, marks time gaily, beating his drum, then pantomimes rolling waves, and great affluence. The king and the princess show surprise and pleasure. The other drummers mark time. The Pretty Drummer repeats his action in line 2.

Rum, tum, tum-ti-ti-tum, I've ships and gold a-plenty."

The entire cast breaks into the sailors' hornpipe.

VERSE 12.

"O drummer boy, then you may wed my daughter,

The king walks between the Pretty Drummer and the princess, joining their hands benevolently. The other drummers march gaily across the stage, changing places.

O drummer boy, then you may wed my daughter,

The king kisses his daughter and clasps the Pretty Drummer on the shoulder. The other drummers go back to their old positions.

Rum tum, tum-ti-ti-tum, then you may wed my daughter."

The king, the princess and the Pretty Drummer join hands and dance around in a circle. The other drummers turn in place.

THE PRETTY DRUMMER

"*My lord and king, I will not wed your daughter,*
The Pretty Drummer strides downstage R., turns, and snaps his fingers at the king, who looks astonished. The princess again applies her handkerchief.

My lord and king, I will not wed your daughter,
The Pretty Drummer continues downstage R., again snapping his fingers. The other drummers imitate the actions of the Pretty Drummer

Rum tum, tum-ti-ti-tum, I will not wed your daughter."
The king and the princess continue to look amazed. The drummers turn in place, and again snap their fingers.

VERSE 14.

"*In my own land we have far fairer maidens,*
In my own land we have far fairer maidens,
The drummers all gaze off R. gesturing romantically, kissing their hands to imaginary maidens elsewhere. The princess weeps on her father's copious chest. The king pats her back sympathetically, rhythmically.

Rum tum, tum-ti-ti-tum, we have far fairer maidens!"
The king and the princess continue as in lines 1–2. The drummers turn in place, and again blow kisses into space.

Conclusion: The chorus sings the first verse very softly. The Pretty Drummer marshalls his companions behind him; the three march off in single file, waving gaily and rather insolently at the king and his daughter. The king stalks out R.; the princess runs off L., weeping into her inadequate pocket-handkerchief.

Adapted from the English version by John Wishart, reprinted from the Clarendon Song Book — 1A, by permission of the Oxford University Press.

XVI. *RATAPLAN*

XVI. RATAPLAN

French
Translated by
Alice M. G. White

1--The drums had called to the king's high throne The drums had called to the king's high throne The la - dies of the whole of France, And the ve - ry first the king be - held Did his deep - est soul en - - - trance. *Refrain:* Rat - a - - plan, rat - a - plan, Rat - a - plan, plan, plan, plan, Rat - a - plan, Rat - a plan, Rat - a - plan, plan, - plan, plan,

XVI. RATAPLAN

2. "Marquis, pray tell me, if thou canst,
   Marquis, pray tell me, if thou canst,
   This most lovely woman's name?"
   "My liege and king, she is my wife,
   Her lot and mine, they are the same."
   Rataplan, etc.

3. "Marquis, thou hast more bliss than I,
   Marquis, thou hast more bliss than I,
   To own a wife who is so rare.
   If thou wouldst grant her unto me
   I'd keep her in my royal care."
   Rataplan, etc.

4. "Sire wert thou not my lord and king,
   Sire wert thou not my lord and king,
   Thy death knell should soon be rung;
   But since thou art my lord and king,
   I use a bridle on my tongue."
   Rataplan, etc.

5. "Marquis, do not distress thyself,
   Marquis, do not distress thyself,
   Straightway I shall thy powers enhance,
   It pleaseth me to create thee
   The Lord High Marshall of all France."
   Rataplan, etc.

149

6. "Array thyself most beauteously,
   Array thyself most beauteously,
   And braid thy lustrous silken hair;
   Array thyself most beauteously
   To be his bidden love so fair."
   Rataplan, etc.

7. "Adieu, my life, adieu, my love,
   Adieu, my life, adieu, my love,
   Adieu, my joy, my hope, my heart.
   Since thou art bound to serve the king,
   In sorrow now we twain must part."
   Rataplan, etc.

8. The queen has made a fair bouquet,
   The queen has made a fair bouquet,
   Of wondrous stately fleur de lys.
   The fatal scent of this bouquet
   Brought death itself to the marquise!
   Rataplan, etc.

According to some authorities the above ballad was sung in reference to King Henry IV of France and Navarre. He was in love with Gabrielle d'Estrées and wished to divorce his wife, Queen Margaret, when the former suddenly died in 1599; the queen was suspected of causing her to be murdered.

XVI. RATAPLAN

PRESENTATION: This is one of the most spectacular of ballads from the dramatic standpoint. It is suffused with irony and works up to a powerful climax. It should be undertaken only after the group has interpreted some of the less complicated dramatizations. The story may be treated almost as if it were a miniature opera, the minor characters singing the narrative in verses 1 and 8, the principals singing their dialogue, and the clown the Rataplan refrains, accompanying himself in reality or in pantomime upon his instrument, except in verse 7.

STAGING: If possible, an elaborate mediaeval setting, to represent the king's throne room. A short flight of steps leads up to the dais on which stand the thrones of the king and queen. The dais is placed diagonally on the left, quite far downstage; for an effective ending a curtain is absolutely necessary. A large bouquet of fleur-de-lys is required in the last verse.

COSTUMING: The king, the queen, the marquis, the marquise, the court ladies, gentlemen, and pages, all wear appropriate mediaeval attire. The jester wears a fantastic parti-colored outfit, and grotesque make-up. He carries a bauble, and a lute or guitar.

ACTION: Facial expression is of vital importance, the principal actors requiring all the subtlety at their command to portray their rôles. The minor personages must show great interest in the situation, interpreting events in the manner of the Greek chorus. Throughout the scene the clown is disregarded by everyone on the stage, but is actually the wisest person there. Reaching out to the audience from the glittering, yet sinister court, he communicates his forebodings of impending disaster. The music in this ballad forms background for the action rather than a vigorous accompaniment and does not call for the stylization suited to the simpler and more humorous examples in this book. The rhythm is

RATAPLAN

smooth and does not need to be greatly accentuated; it is a flowing accompaniment for significant action and the subtle evolution of the tragedy.

INTRODUCTION: A trumpeter should come in smartly from R. (all entrances and exits occur on this side), take up a position at back centre, and sound a flourish. Several page boys enter and group themselves round the dais. The king and queen then appear, followed by the clown and a few courtiers, including the marquis. The royal pair seat themselves on their thrones, the queen on the king's left; the jester crouches on the lowest steps of the dais, near the audience; the courtiers group themselves round the stage, the marquis standing to the king's right. A drummer boy marches importantly in, stands beside the trumpeter, and beats a loud tattoo.

VERSE 1. The ladies enter, walking gracefully and rhythmically in twos and threes, they move in the direction of the thrones, in front of which each makes a deep curtsey, proceeding counterclockwise round the room to designated positions upstage and on the right. The marquise is the first to make her obeisance then she goes round to the right, stopping in a prominent position downstage, where she stands conversing (silently) with a courtier, in the direct line of vision of the king, who appears spellbound by her beauty, though he perfunctorily acknowledges the homage of the other ladies. The queen inclines her head indifferently to the subjects, but senses her husband's incipient disaffection and watches him covertly. The clown amuses himself by surveying the arrival of the guests, playing with his bauble, and appearing to comment on the court ladies to the audience, and on the king's new interest.

Refrain. Picking up his lute he pantomimes, or actually plays his own accompaniment, and sings the "rataplans" gaily, yet mockingly.

RATAPLAN

VERSE 2. The courtiers converse in groups, while the king beckons to the marquis, gestures towards the marquise, and sings his question, during lines 1 and 2. In lines 3 and 4 the marquis makes reply with obvious pride. Throughout the verse the queen remains motionless, and almost expressionless, yet manages to convey to the audience by the look in her eyes, her own sense of insecurity. The clown listens intently and communicates a feeling of apprehension.

Refrain. A certain tenseness has now crept into his tone as he sings and strums.

VERSE 3. The courtiers move about the stage unobtrusively, and carry on their silent conversation. Several of the gentlemen pay their attentive addresses to the marquise who is unconscious of being the subject of royal interest. The king sings the verse confidentially, yet audibly, putting his hand on the shoulder of the marquis and looking at him. The marquis appears outraged, puts his hand on the hilt of his sword, and makes an involuntary movement towards the king. The queen gives a start, restrains herself, though with difficulty, and turns away from the king in mortification. The clown listens with even greater apprehension than in the last verse.

Refrain. In a vain attempt to forestall events he sings his "rataplans" urgently and warningly, but no one takes any notice.

VERSE 4. Recovering himself, the marquis sings proudly, yet sadly; the king listens tolerantly. The queen broods silently, darting vindictive glances at the marquise. The clown, almost unable to contain himself, scrambles round in front of the throne, stretching himself out near the king's feet, looking into the face of the marquis, then at the king.

Refrain. Still in this position, he sings his "rataplans" commiseratingly.

VERSE 5. The king sings his lines suavely. During line 2 he rises, and summons the marquis to a kneeling position in front of him. During line 3 the marquis kneels reluctantly and in line 4 receives a decoration from the king. The clown shrinks back to his former position on the dais, his head sinking dejectedly in his hands. The queen, with murder in her heart, watches the bestowal of the honor. Suddenly the whole assemblage realizes that a ceremony is taking place. While the king is speaking there is an attitude of animation, the marquise appearing particularly delighted.

Refrain. Looking up at the king, who ignores him, the clown sings with bitter condemnation. Head held high, the queen rises, descends from her throne, and sweeps out during the first half of the refrain. The courtiers make way for her, surprised at her sudden departure. The marquis, during the second part of the refrain, strides over to his wife.

VERSE 6. Putting his arm round her he touches her hair lovingly, sings tenderly, looking into her eyes, and then glances with hatred at the king. The courtiers exchange furtive looks, and watch proceedings intently. The king sits down, well satisfied at the result of his strategy. The clown watches the marquis and his wife, shaking his head miserably.

Refrain. Pityingly the clown sings his song, the rest of the court reflecting his emotion. The king, self-satisfied, continues to smile. The marquis and marquise embrace.

VERSE 7. The marquise sings the verse as she looks adoringly at her husband. The courtiers, moved by pity and fear draw closer together, the men as if to protect their wives, several of whom shed tears of sympathy. The king rises during the last line of the verse.

RATAPLAN

The clown is prostrate with grief, having rolled over on his face across the steps.

Refrain. In this position the clown moans the refrain to himself in a heartbroken fashion, as the marquis leads his wife over to the dais. She mounts the steps, reluctantly accepting the hand of the king, who motions her into the queen's throne, on which she sits. He also seats himself and gazes at her rapturously.

VERSE 8. A page enters carrying a beautiful bouquet. Kneeling before the marquise he presents it to her at the end of line 2. She receives it courteously, smelling the flowers with pleasure, in line 3. All express interest at the arrival of the flowers. During the last line the marquise gives a convulsive shudder and sinks back on her chair, dead. As she dies, all stand horror stricken, except for the clown who remains on the steps, gazing at the lady with a piteous expression.

Refrain. The king leans over the dead marquise in an attempt to revive her. He is thrust aside by the marquis, who dashes forward and supports the lifeless body in his arms. Utter horror grips the entire court. The clown utters his "rataplans" in a hysterical crescendo rising almost to a shriek on the high notes and ending in a sob on the last notes.

CURTAIN

XVII. *TANCUJ*

XVII. TANCUJ

(DANCE)

Gaily   Czechoslovakian

1– "Stamp and dance, be nim - ble and

mer - ry, But watch the stove, do try to be

wa - ry, For you must know I have no warm

bed, And when it's cold I need it in -

Chorus:

stead." Tra la la la, Tra la

ritard second time

la la, la la la la la la la la la la la la

XVII. TANCUJ

2. "Sentry duty, midnight till morn,
   Ragged, shiv'ring, why was I born?
   Amid the rain I pace, keeping guard,
   A soldier's life is weary and hard."
   Tra la la, etc.

3. "Tell me, gypsy, have I a lover?
   Oh, is there someone I can discover?"
   "My pretty maid, cross my hand with gold,
   Your future then, at once I'll unfold!"
   Tra la la, etc.

4. "Rise up, husband, why do you loll here?
   You've done no work for many a long year."
   "Why should I work when life is so short?
   This, old wife, is my final retort!"
   Tra la la, etc.

XVII. TANCUJ

PRESENTATION: This Czechoslovakian folksong is full of color and gaiety. Great informality characterizes it, for the verses have no narrative connecting them and a lively refrain affords opportunity for dancing and merriment between the stanzas. This informality is accentuated if a soloist, attired in Slavic peasant costume, sings the verses, while the actors join in for the refrain.

STAGING: A stove, or a fire-place (on which is a frying pan), should occupy the stage at the back centre; on either side of it is a wooden bench.

COSTUMING: The women wear brightly colored peasant skirts and blouses, kerchiefs, and gaily embroidered aprons; the gypsy in verse 3 should wear large earrings, heavy bracelets and necklaces; the chief character in verse 1 should be represented as a middle-aged housewife, while the woman in the last verse should be untidy and dirty-looking, as should her husband.

ACTION: The relationship between the actors and the audience is very intimate. The solo singer may stand on one side of the stage, accompanying his singing with a guitar, banjo, or similar instrument. As each verse ends, the actors dance; afterwards they need not leave the stage, but may remain to watch the action for each succeeding verse, all joining in a general dance for the "grand finale."

VERSE 1.
> *"Stamp and dance, be nimble and merry,*

Enter from R. the house-wife, beckoning to R. and L. She goes to the centre of the stage. She is followed by a peasant boy and girl, while from stage L. another couple enter. They are gay and carefree. They stand on either side of her.

TANCUJ

But watch the stove, do try to be wary,
The housewife shakes her finger at the young people, then makes
a gesture towards the stove. The girls and boys nod, laughing to
one another.

>*For you must know I have no warm bed,*
>*And when it's cold I need it instead."*

The housewife pretends to be sad, shivers violently, and turns
gratefully to the stove again. The young people laugh and prepare
to dance.

Chorus.
>*Tra la la, etc.*

The four step forward and dance. Great variety is possible, any
number of Slavic dances * being available for the purpose. The
dance may be long or short according to the desires of the partici-
pants. The chorus may be repeated any number of times.

* "The Little Butcher," from "Ten Slavic Dances" by Marjorie Crane Geary,
(Woman's Press) is a particularly effective dance and the directions are easy
to comprehend.

The housewife stands in front of her stove, smiling at the dancers
and clapping her hands. After the dance, one couple saunters over
to R., the other to stage L., smiling and conversing (silently), ready
to watch the next "scene." The housewife sits on the bench L., re-
maining there throughout the ballad, enjoying events as they pass
before her.

VERSE 2.
>*"Sentry duty, midnight till morn,*
>*Ragged, shiv'ring, why was I born?*

Enter from L. a soldier carrying a rifle on his shoulder. He marches

TANCUJ

wearily across the stage for seven steps, making an about-turn on the last note of line 2.

Amid the rain I pace keeping guard,
A soldier's life is weary and hard.

He marches back for seven steps, shivering, turning up his collar, wrapping his threadbare coat about him. He makes an about-turn on the last note of line 4.

Chorus.

Tra la la, etc.

The peasant girls and boys repeat their dance. The soldier marches up and down as in verse 2, this time with a lively air. The housewife beats time while the dance proceeds. At the end of the chorus the dancers again stand on either side of the stage; the soldier joins one pair. All watch the events of verse 3. Towards the end of the chorus the gypsy enters from R., and sits on the bench R.

VERSE 3.

"Tell me, gypsy, have I a lover?
Oh, is there someone I can discover?"

From L. comes a young peasant girl, who approaches the gypsy eagerly, and kneels beside her.

"My pretty maid, cross my hand with gold,

The gypsy holds out her hand; the girl gives her some coins.

Your future then, at once I'll unfold!"

The gypsy proceeds to describe a handsome man, with moustachios, sleek hair, and noble bearing. The girl listens entranced.

Chorus.

Tra la la, etc.

The peasants dance, the soldier marches up and down, the house-

TANCUJ

wife claps her hands, the gypsy and the girl move downstage R. where the gypsy spreads out fortune-telling cards on the floor and commences to read the girl's future. At the end of the chorus the actors take up their former positions, excepting the gypsy and the girl, who continue as in the chorus. Toward the end of the chorus the gypsy man, a big ungainly creature, enters from R., and sprawls in front of the stove.

VERSE 4.

> *"Rise up, husband, why do you loll here?*

Enter abruptly from R. the gypsy's spouse, sweeping the floor with a broom.

> *You've done no work for many a long year."*

She pokes her man with the broom, and tries unsuccessfully to pull him to his feet.

> *"Why should I work when life is so short?*

He rises suddenly, seizing the frying pan from the stove; she backs away from him in dismay.

> *This, old wife, is my final retort!"*

He whacks her soundly across the rear with the frying pan, on the word "this," and chases her round in a circle.

Chorus.

> *Tra la la, etc.*

The peasant girls and boys dance, the housewife claps her hands, the soldier marches gaily up and down, the gypsy continues to tell the young girl's fortune, the gypsy couple chase one another round the stage. At the end of the dance the whole cast joins hands in a large ring, dancing round gaily. One character leads the company off, either to the right or left. It is amusing to leave the wife and husband at the end of the procession, the latter going off with a final flip of the frying pan at his wife's disappearing form.

XVIII. *THREE PIRATES*

XVIII. THREE PIRATES

With spirit　　　　　　　　　　　　　　　　　　　　English

1– Three pir - ates came to Lon - don Town, Yo

ho, - - - - Yo ho, - - - - Three

pir - ates came to Lon - don Town, Yo

ho, - - - - Yo ho, - - - - Three

pir - ates came to Lon - don Town, To

see the king put on his crown. Yo

Refrain:

ho, you lub - bers, Yo ho, you lub - bers, Yo

ho, Yo ho, Yo ho.

XVIII. THREE PIRATES

2. At first they came to a wayside inn, Yo ho, Yo ho,
   At first they came to a wayside inn, Yo ho, Yo ho,
   At first they came to a wayside inn,
   And said, "Good landlord, let us in."
   Yo ho, you lubbers, etc.

3. "Oh, landlord, have you good red wine, Yo ho, Yo ho,
   "Oh, landlord, have you good red wine, Yo ho, Yo ho,
   "Oh, landlord, have you good red wine,
      Enough to fill this cask of mine?"
   Yo ho, you lubbers, etc.

4. "Oh, yes, sirs, I have good red wine, Yo ho, Yo ho,
   "Oh, yes, sirs, I have good red wine, Yo ho, Yo ho,
   "Oh, yes, sirs, I have good red wine,
      Enough to fill this cask of thine."
   Yo ho, you lubbers, etc.

5. "Oh, landlord, have you bags of gold, Yo ho, Yo ho,
   "Oh, landlord, have you bags of gold, Yo ho, Yo ho,
   "Oh, landlord, have you bags of gold,
      Enough to fill the after-hold?"
   Yo ho, you lubbers, etc.

6. "Oh, yes, sirs, I have bags of gold, Yo ho, Yo ho,
   "Oh, yes, sirs, I have bags of gold, Yo ho, Yo ho,
   "Oh, yes, sirs, I have bags of gold,
      Enough to fill the after-hold."
   Yo ho, you lubbers, etc.

7. "Oh, landlord, have you a daughter fair, Yo ho, Yo ho,
   "Oh, landlord, have you a daughter fair, Yo ho, Yo ho,
   "Oh, landlord, have you a daughter fair,
   With laughing eyes and curly hair?"
   Yo ho, you lubbers, etc.

8. "Oh, yes, sirs, I've a daughter fair, Yo ho, Yo ho,
   "Oh, yes, sirs, I've a daughter fair, Yo ho, Yo ho,
   "Oh, yes, sirs, I've a daughter fair,
   With laughing eyes and curly hair."
   Yo ho, you lubbers, etc.

9. "Oh, landord, will she marry me, Yo ho, Yo ho,
   "Oh, landlord, will she marry me, Yo ho, Yo ho,
   "Oh, landlord, will she marry me,
   And sail with me across the sea?"
   Yo ho, you lubbers, etc.

10. "Oh, yes, sirs, she will marry thee, Yo ho, Yo ho,
    "Oh, yes, sirs, she will marry thee, Yo ho, Yo ho,
    "Oh, yes, sirs, she will marry thee,
    And sail with thee across the sea."
    Yo ho, you lubbers, etc.

XVIII. THREE PIRATES

PRESENTATION: This ballad with its rollicking rhythm invites general participation. A chorus may sing it throughout (the more, the merrier), the audience joining in the "yo ho's," while the players silently portray the action.

STAGING: The stage represents the interior of an inn; at back centre is a fireplace, with, if possible, a cheerful blaze in it, and stools on either side. On the left, upstage, is a door leading to another part of the hostelry and also on left, downstage, a table with several chairs or benches round it. Other realistic touches may be added. Downstage R. is the inn "front door." Some tankards are necessary, an empty cask, and some fat and convincing-looking money bags. Steps lead from the auditorium up to the extreme right of the stage.

COSTUMING: The pirates have enormous sea-boots, colored breeches, shirts and sashes, wide slouch hats, worn at jaunty angles, and murderous-looking weapons sticking in their waistbands. Voluminous cloaks hang from their shoulders; they sport large earrings and fierce moustachios. Two of them are of decidedly villainous appearance, but one, the leader, must be attractive in a swashbuckling way. The girls are attired in the skirts and bodices of old-time simple country-maids; the older sisters wear their clothes badly, and make their hair look rather unattractive by straining it back or letting it fall lank and straight. The youngest sister is neat and coquettish, and must have curly hair, its charm accentuated by a bright ribbon tied round it. Mine host has a dark shirt, breeches and hose, and wears a large white apron; it adds to the comic effect if he is a bit bow-legged!

ACTION: The rhythm must be strongly accented throughout. The players should use sweeping gestures and swaggering attitudes, piratical overstatement being a positive virtue! An entry from the back of the hall and up the centre aisle to the stage, induces a feeling of intimacy between audience and cast.

THREE PIRATES

The pirates, entering from the rear, march the length of the hall. The first and second twirl their moustaches as they walk, toss the ends of their cloaks over their shoulders, and make other grandiose gestures. The third pirate follows them carrying an empty wine-cask on his shoulder; their strides are large, their demeanour fierce and proud. They must time their entry so as to arrive at the foot of the stage steps at the end of the verse.

VERSE 2.

> *At first they came to a wayside inn, Yo ho, Yo ho,*

The leader looks surprised, then points out the inn to his companions on the "yo ho's," twice, with vigor.

> *At first they came to a wayside inn, Yo ho, Yo ho,*

The second and third pirates repeat his gestures.

> *At first they came to a wayside inn*

Rhythmically and gleefully they mount the steps, urging one another along.

> *And said, "Good landlord, let us in."*

The singers pause on words "let us in," and the pirate leader bangs peremptorily on the inn "door."

> ### Refrain

On the first two "yo ho, you lubbers" the landlord enters from L., and crosses the floor quickly to admit his guests (he makes all his entrances and exits from L.). On the three final "yo ho's" the pirates enter the inn impatiently.

VERSE 3.

> *"Oh, landlord, have you good red wine, Yo ho, Yo ho,*

The third pirate takes three steps towards the centre, downstage, puts down cask on the word "wine," and stretches his "stiff" arm twice on the "yo ho's." The two other men look around menacingly. The landlord shrinks back towards the table for seven

steps, somewhat scared, but trying to cover his fear because he
hopes for custom.

Oh, landlord, have you good red wine, Yo ho, Yo ho,

The pirates take four strides over to the fire-place and on the first
"yo ho" throw their hats down on the stools; on the second "yo ho"
their cloaks follow. Turning their backs to the fire, they stand with
feet wide apart.

Oh, landlord, have you good red wine

Standing thus in a row the men make a lordly questioning motion
to the innkeeper who remains petrified by the table.

Enough to fill this cask of mine?"

They point to the cask.

Refrain

They take four large steps over to the chairs round the table while
the innkeeper backs off the stage. On the first "yo ho" the leader
seats himself heavily, then the second pirate, and the third on the
last "yo ho." They sit with legs outstretched in masculine fashion.

Verse 4.

"Oh, yes, sirs, I have good red wine, Yo ho, Yo ho,

The innkeeper enters with a tankard of wine and takes three steps
to the table. On the word "wine" he places the vessel in front of the
first pirate. On the "yo ho's" he makes his exit, while the first pirate
flourishes the tankard in the air.

Oh, yes, sirs, I have good red wine, Yo ho, Yo ho,

As above, the landlord re-enters with two tankards and places them
before the second and third pirates. They all wave tankards in the
air on the "yo ho's."

Oh yes, sirs, I have good red wine

The innkeeper takes four steps over to the cask.

Enough to fill this cask of thine."

THREE PIRATES

He lifts it and walks out with it, as he nods deprecatingly to his "customers."

Refrain

The pirates pledge one another's health on "yo ho, you lubbers," and toss off their drinks with heads thrown back, on the final "yo ho's."

VERSE 5.

>*"Oh, landlord, have you bags of gold, Yo ho, Yo ho,*

Excited by the wine, the leader pantomimes shouting at the innkeeper through left exit.

>*Oh, landlord, have you bags of gold, Yo ho, Yo ho,*

The second and third pirates repeat the gesture.

>*Oh, landlord, have you bags of gold,*

The landlord enters, taking four steps to the table, looking terrified.

>*Enough to fill the afterhold?"*

The pirates make a gesture signifying the size of the after-hold and look intimidating.

.Refrain

The innkeeper retires precipitately. The pirates bang on the table with closed fists, on the "ho's."

VERSE 6.

>*"Oh, yes, sirs, I have bags of gold, Yo ho, Yo ho,*

The landlord enters, carrying bags of gold. Looking dejected, he takes three steps towards the fireplace, depositing his burden on the floor on the word "gold," while the pirates watch him. On the "yo ho's," he makes his exit and the pirates gesture exuberantly.

>*Oh, yes, sirs, I have bags of gold, Yo ho, Yo ho,*

Repeat the action for line one, the innkeeper looking more crestfallen.

THREE PIRATES

> *Oh, yes, sirs, I have bags of gold*

As above, till word "gold."

> *Enough to fill the after-hold."*

The innkeeper stands looking dismally at the money bags and shakes his head sadly in rhythm. The pirates appear even more jovial.

Refrain

The robbers lean towards one another with an air of conspiracy on "yo ho, you lubbers." On the last "yo ho's," they throw back their heads as if laughing heartily.

VERSE 7.

> *"Oh, landlord, have you a daughter fair, Yo ho, Yo ho,*

The leader beckons imperiously to the host. The latter takes four reluctant steps towards the table on the "yo ho's."

> *Oh, landlord, have you a daughter fair, Yo ho, Yo ho,*

The pirates pantomime questioning him as he stands before them. On the "yo ho's" they gesture airily.

> *Oh, landlord, have you a daughter fair*

They question more pressingly.

> *With laughing eyes and curly hair?"*

They make motions suggestive of laughing eyes and curly hair.

Refrain

The innkeeper makes his exit, nodding to himself rhythmically, smoothing his face as if coming to a decision. The pirates drink, and clink their tankards, on the last "yo ho's."

VERSE 8.

> *"Oh, yes, sirs, I've a daughter fair, Yo ho, Yo ho,*

The chorus, to be literal, *may* take a slight liberty with the song and sing, "Oh yes, sirs, I have *daughters* fair" in this line and the next. The landlord enters eagerly with the two homely older daughters as the pirates rise expectantly. The father conducts the two girls, taking four smart paces, over to the fireplace, leaving one on each side of it, whence they try to glance archly at the free-booters. The father looks ingratiating; the pirates appraise the girls coolly. The chorus sing the "yo ho's" slowly and doubtfully.

Oh, yes, sirs, I've a daughter fair, Yo ho, Yo ho,
The innkeeper takes four steps towards the pirates as if to convince them of his daughters' desirability. The chorus sing even more hesitatingly as the pirates shake their heads four times. On the "yo ho's" the singers recover the tempo, the pirates wave their weapons at the host, who looks desperate.

Oh, yes, sirs, I've a daughter fair
Completely over-awed he nods his head three times, emphatically, and the pirates put down their weapons.

With laughing eyes and curly hair."
He makes gestures depicting the third daughter's extreme come-liness.

Refrain
The landlord makes hasty exit. The pirates slap their thighs in time with the music, looking eagerly offstage L. The older sisters glance at each other ruefully.

Refrain, loudly repeated.
The innkeeper enters with his third daughter, taking four steps over to the fireplace, where he deposits her between her sisters. She stands with eyes modestly downcast; the pirates look entranced. On the "yo ho's" the host takes three more steps across stage and stands R., in a line with the pirates and opposite them.

VERSE 9.

"Oh, landlord, will she marry me, Yo ho, Yo ho,
The second pirate takes one step towards stage R. and pantomimes

asking the landlord for the hand of his youngest daughter, designating her, and then pointing to himself on the word "me." He bows low on the first "yo ho" and straightens himself on the second. The girls look highly interested; the father shakes his head decisively, twice.

Oh, landlord, will she marry me, Yo ho, Yo ho,
The third pirate advances two steps, then the action proceeds as above. The girls still register great attention.

Oh, landlord, will she marry me
The leader pushes past his fellows, takes four eager strides towards the landlord, pointing to himself on the word "me."

And sail with me across the sea?"
All three pirates make rolling motion from L. to R. with their arms outstretched and moving rhythmically.

Refrain

The host and the pirates are now across the stage in this order, from R. to L. Host, first pirate, third pirate, second pirate. Facing front they all do a hornpipe step.

VERSE 10.
"Oh, yes, sirs, she will marry thee, Yo ho, Yo ho,
The landlord takes four steps to nearer elder daughter, takes her by the hand, and on the "Yo ho's" conducts her to the third pirate, who looks resignedly at the audience, with an almost imperceptible sigh, then bows to the girl on the second "yo ho."

Oh, yes, sirs, she will marry thee, Yo ho, Yo ho,
As above with the second sister and the second pirate.

Oh, yes, sirs, she will marry thee
The youngest daughter trips shyly over to the leader; the father takes four steps back towards stage L., standing between the table

and the audience he looks bewildered at her willingness. The pirate
leader is charmed.

> *And sail with thee across the sea."*

The girls gesture rolling waves, looking happy at the thought of
adventure. The men smile at them approvingly.

Refrain

The couples hold hands and dance in three circles.

VERSE I. Repeat rather softly.

> *Three pirates came to London Town, Yo ho, Yo ho,*

The pirates turn, walk over to fire-stools in four steps, pick up
their hats and cloaks on the "yo ho's." They stand upstage in a row.

> *Three pirates came to London Town, Yo ho, Yo ho,*

The father walks across the stage, along the line of his daughters,
and kisses them in turn on the words "London," "ho" and "ho."

> *Three pirates came to London Town*

The pirates march forward three paces and each puts an arm
round his girl so that she is on his left. The host takes four steps
across towards stage L.

> *To see the king put on his crown.*

With sweeping disdainful gestures, the buccaneers motion to the
host that he can keep his wine and money bags. The latter looks
staggered by the vagaries of Fortune (and pirates).

Refrain

The couples go off dancing through inn-door R., waving joyously
at the audience. The innkeeper picks up one tankard listlessly and
goes out L. as in a daze, scratching his head.

(In this particular ballad the players may have to modify the action
according to the size of the stage. The landlord has much to do,
and his bustling is typical of his highly nervous state; if, however,
he cannot reach the places designated in the above scheme, extra
music could be inserted to allow him more time.)

XIX. THE WEE COOPER O' FIFE

XIX. THE WEE COOPER
O' FIFE

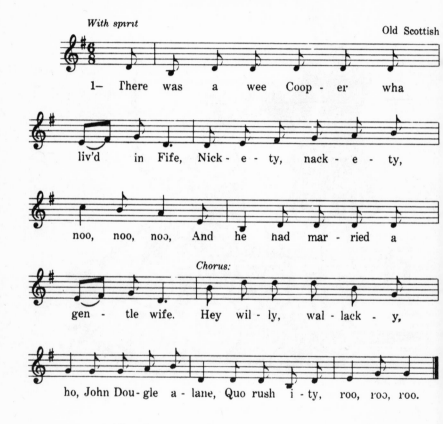

With spirit   Old Scottish

1— There was a wee Coop - er wha liv'd in Fife, Nick - e - ty, nack - e - ty, noo, noo, noo, And he had mar - ried a gen - tle wife.

Chorus:

Hey wil - ly, wal - lack - y, ho, John Dou - gle a - lane, Quo rush i - ty, roo, roo, roo.

XIX. THE WEE COOPER O' FIFE

2. She wad na bake, nor wad she brew,
   Nickety, nackety, noo, noo, noo.
   For spilin' o' her comely hue.
   Hey willy wallacky, etc.

3. She wad na caird, nor wad she spin,
   Nickety, nackety, noo, noo, noo.
   For shamin' o' her gentle kin:
   Hey willy wallacky, etc.

4. The Cooper has gone to his woo' pack,
   Nickety, nackety, noo, noo, noo.
   And he's laid a sheep's skin on his wife's back;
   Hey willy wallacky, etc.

5. I'll no be shamin' your gentle kin,
   Nickety, nackety, noo, noo, noo.
   But I will skelp my ain sheepskin,
   Hey willy wallacky, etc.

6. O I will bake and I will brew,
   Nickety, nackety, noo, noo, noo.
   And think nae mair o' my comely hue;
   Hey willy wallacky, etc.

7. O I will wash and I will spin,
   Nickety, nackety, noo, noo, noo.
   And think nae mair o' my gentle kin;
   Hey willy wallacky, etc.

XIX. THE WEE COOPER O' FIFE

PRESENTATION: A reader may recite the entire poem, or merely the narrative parts, while the players say the dialogue lines. The music, however, is sprightly, and when sung by a chorus forms a gay background for the action. This last method has been used in the following description.

STAGING: The setting is very simple. A small bench, or a stool, occupies the centre of the stage. A chest, from which the cooper extracts his sheepskin, stands at the back centre. The sheepskin should be a real one, if possible,— otherwise a piece of cloth cut in imitation of the actual thing. It should have a noose attached so that it may be slipped over the wife's head.

COSTUMING: The cooper should, if possible, wear a kilt, and a tam o'shanter. The wife wears a skirt, a bodice, and a little shawl.

ACTION: The action is lively, the cooper moving briskly in a cocksure manner.

VERSE I.

> *There was a wee Cooper wha liv'd in Fife,*
> *Nickety, nackety, noo, noo, noo,*

The cooper enters from R., conducting his wife to the centre of the stage. They take up a position in front of the bench, having walked for seven steps.

> *And he had married a gentle wife.*

The wife makes a deep curtsy; the cooper stands regarding her in admiration.

Chorus.   *Hey willy wallacky, etc.*

The cooper and his wife do a dance step during the first line; during the second, he conveys her to the bench. She sits as the music ends; he stands looking at her.

THE WEE COOPER O' FIFE

She wad na bake, nor wad she brew,

The cooper, with a surprised look on his face, pantomimes baking, then brewing. A change comes over the wife; she shakes her head emphatically, and of course, rhythmically.

Nickety, nackety, noo, noo, noo,

The cooper looks very much surprised, puzzled, and angry. His wife continues to toss her head.

For spilin' o' her comely hue.

The wife takes a little mirror from her pocket, and admires herself in it. The cooper taps his foot on the floor, impatiently.

Chorus.   Hey willy wallacky, etc.

The cooper crosses in front of his wife to stage R., taking seven angry steps, turning to regard her with misgivings on the last note of the chorus. The wife sits preening herself, fussing with her shawl, bonnet, hair, face and hands.

VERSE 3.   *She wad na caird, nor wad she spin,*

The cooper pantomimes carding wool, and spinning. His wife shakes her head rhythmically.

Nickety, nackety, noo, noo, noo,

The cooper shows great indignation, tearing his hair, stamping his foot. The wife repeats her proud denials.

For shamin' o' her gentle kin:

The wife looks up to heaven, raising her hands in horror. The cooper shakes his fist at her four times.

Chorus.   Hey willy wallacky, etc.

The wife rises, skips round the bench, tossing her head, and sits again, as the music ends. The cooper stalks angrily across the stage from R. to L. Each takes seven steps.

THE WEE COOPER O' FIFE

The cooper has gone to his woo' pack,
Nickety, nackety, noo, noo, noo,

The cooper, indicating (on the word "cooper") that he has a good idea, winks at the audience, turns and walks upstage, behind the bench on which his wife sits prinking. He takes six steps. On the last note of line 2 he stoops, and picks up the sheepskin from the chest.

And he's laid a sheep's skin on his wife's back;

The cooper takes three big strides over to his wife, slipping the noose of the sheepskin over his wife's head and laying the skin on her back, on the last note of the line. The wife shrugs and wriggles rhythmically.

Chorus.   *Hey willy wallacky, etc.*

The wife continues to shrug and wriggle. The cooper grins vindictively, seizes a stick from the floor (back centre), and, grinning expectantly, prepares to beat his wife.

VERSE 5.

I'll no be shamin' you gentle kin,
Nickety, nackety, noo, noo, noo,
But I will skelp my ain sheepskin,

The cooper pantomimes hitting her a powerful blow, on the word "no." She rises suddenly, but he holds on to her, and continues to beat her. It is important that the blows fall at regular intervals, and that the wife shrink away from them, also in rhythm. The cooper may leap over the bench during line 1, and continue the beating from in front of it.

Chorus.   *Hey willy wallacky, etc.*

The cooper chases his wife round the bench, beating her with his stick. She sinks exhausted on the floor in front of the bench, on the last note of the chorus music. The cooper takes up a position on stage L. looking triumphant.

THE WEE COOPER O' FIFE

O I will bake and I will brew,

On her knees, the wife pleads with the cooper, pantomiming baking and brewing. He folds his arms, turning away from her, smiling to himself, satisfied.

Nickety, nackety, noo, noo, noo,
And think nae mair o' my comely hue;

He continues, as in line 1. She pleads, still on her knees, pantomiming her disregard of her fair complexion.

Chorus.   Hey willy wallacky, etc.

She sobs and cries, her shoulders heaving convulsively to the rhythm of the music. He stalks over to stage R. as though reluctant to yield, and stands quite still on the last note of the chorus music.

Verse 7.

O I will wash and I will spin,

The wife pantomimes washing and spinning. The cooper turns and listens attentively, nodding his head in satisfaction.

Nickety, nackety, noo, noo, noo,

The cooper walks pompously over to her.

And think nae mair o' my gentle kin;

The cooper raises his wife from the ground, kissing her in forgiveness, on the word "kin." She shows great penitence.

Chorus.   Hey willy wallacky, etc.

They take hands and skip off R., waving to the audience as they gaily make their exit.

XX. WHERE ARE YOU GOING TO, MY PRETTY MAID?

XX. WHERE ARE YOU GOING MY PRETTY MAID?

Brightly   English

1 "Where are you go - ing to, my pret - ty maid?" "I'm go - ing a - milk - ing, sir," she said, "Sir," she said, "sir," she said, "I'm go - ing a - milk - ing, sir," she said.

XX. WHERE ARE YOU GOING TO,
MY PRETTY MAID?

2. "May I go with you, my pretty maid?"
   "You're kindly welcome, sir," she said,
   "Sir," she said, "Sir," she said,
   "You're kindly welcome, sir," she said.

3. "What is your father, my pretty maid?"
   "My father's a farmer, sir," she said,
   "Sir," she said, "Sir," she said,
   "My father's a farmer, sir," she said.

4. "Say, will you marry me, my pretty maid?"
   "Yes, if you please, kind sir," she said,
   "Sir," she said, "Sir," she said,
   "Yes, if you please, kind sir," she said.

5. "What is your fortune, my pretty maid?"
   "My face is my fortune, sir," she said,
   "Sir," she said, "Sir," she said,
   "My face is my fortune, sir," she said.

6. "Then I won't marry you, my pretty maid,"
   "Nobody asked you, sir," she said,
   "Sir," she said, "Sir," she said,
   "Nobody asked you, sir," she said.

XX. WHERE ARE YOU GOING TO,

PRESENTATION: This ballad may be acted very simply by two characters, the man and the maid, or by two or more couples performing the action simultaneously and in perfect unison. The following arrangement has been worked out for two couples. A chorus sings the song while the players interpret it.

STAGING: The stage represents a country road. No properties are necessary, though the milkmaids may carry pails.

COSTUMING: The girls are dressed as simple English country maids of the eighteenth century, with sunbonnets. The men, in contrast, sport rakish town clothes of the same period.

ACTION: Before the first verse is sung the chorus hums the music once through. (It sounds better if they actually sing "la" for each note, as humming does not carry very well.)

INTRODUCTION: *Lines 1–2*

The maidens enter from L. downstage; they trip gaily across towards R. one after the other. The men enter from R. upstage; they proceed across towards L., smiling admiringly at the girls. Each character takes seven steps, halting on the eighth beat of the music.   *Lines 3–4*

The maids take a slip step to one side, a slip step to the other side, turning in place for four steps as the music ends. They hold out their skirts. The men take three steps towards each other, whisper together, then advance in three steps towards the maidens, as the music ends. The four are now standing in a row; maid, man, man, maid.

VERSE 1.

> *"Where are you going to, my pretty maid?"*

The men raise their hats and bow, asking the question with their eyes.

> *"I'm going a-milking sir," she said.*

The maidens rhythmically pantomime milking a cow.

MY PRETTY MAID?

> *"Sir," she said, "Sir," she said,*
> *"I'm going a-milking, sir," she said.*

The girls do the dance step, as in the introduction; the men watch them archly.

VERSE 2.

> *"May I go with you, my pretty maid?"*

The men indicate by a gesture the direction they might take.

> *"You're kindly welcome, sir," she said,*

The girls curtsy.

> *"Sir," she said, "sir," she said,*
> *"You're kindly welcome, sir," she said.*

Each man puts his arm round his maid's waist, and directs her round and upstage; they all take positions facing front, several paces upstage.

VERSE 3.

> *"What is your father, my pretty maid?"*

The men pantomime stroking long beards.

> *"My father's a farmer, sir," she said,*

The maidens pantomime digging.

> *"Sir," she said, "sir," she said,*
> *"My father's a farmer, sir," she said.*

All do a dance step, the maids taking the men's hands, and pirouetting round in a circle.

VERSE 4.

> *"Say, will you marry me, my pretty maid?"*

The men kneel, right hands on their hearts,

> *"Yes, if you please, kind sir," she said,*

The maids curtsy.

> *"Sir," she said, "sir," she said,*

"Yes, if you please, kind sir," she said.

All dance, each couple joining hands and tripping round together.

VERSE 5.

"What is your fortune, my pretty maid?"

The men pantomime rubbing coins together.

"My face is my fortune, sir," she said,

The maids make low curtsies, with right forefingers under their chins.

"Sir," she said, "sir," she said,

The maidens dance; the men frown.

"My face is my fortune, sir," she said.

The maids curtsy as in line 2.

VERSE 6.

"Then I won't marry you, my pretty maid,"

The men turn their backs on the girls, taking three steps towards each other.

"Nobody asked you, sir," she said,

The maids take three steps after them, hands on hips. They snap their fingers at the men on the word "said."

"Sir," she said, "sir," she said,

The maids skip to L. three steps, hands on hips.

"Nobody asked you, sir," she said.

The girls snap their fingers and skip off L. The men look astonished.

Conclusion: The chorus quietly "la-la's" the music through once.

Line 1

The men take three skipping steps after the maids, looking after them blankly.

Line 2

They laugh heartily.

Lines 3–4

They shrug their shoulders and swagger off R.

SUPPLEMENTARY LIST

OF BALLADS AND SONGS, WITH MUSIC

Suitable for Acting

SOURCES

I'm Seventeen come Sunday
Keys of Canterbury, The
My Man John
O no John
Wraggle Taggle Gypsies, The
Brennan on the Moor

Folk Songs, Shanties and
Singing Games. Cecil Sharp.
(H. W. Gray, N. Y., N. Y.)

In Bibberley Town
Old Man Can't Keep his Wife
    at Home, The
Roving Jack
Strawberry Fair
Week's Work Well Done, A

Songs of the West. Baring-
Gould and others.
(Methuen and Co. Ltd., London)

Annie, the Miller's Daughter
Three Rascals, The
Uninvited Aunt, The

Botsford Collection of Folk
Songs. (G. Schirmer, N. Y., N. Y.)

Lord Bateman
Robin Hood and the Tanner

100 English Folk Songs. Cecil
Sharp. (Oliver Ditson, Boston)

Bold Dragoon, The
Roving Journey-Man, The

Songs and Ballads of the West.
Baring Gould and Fleetwood
Sheppard. (Methuen and Co. London)

Miracle of Saint Nicholas, The
Sleeping Princess, The

Concord Series. No. 14
Concord Series. No. 7
(E. C. Schirmer, Boston)

Sir Eglamore
Wiltshire Wedding. The

Oxford Song Book. Vol. 2
(Oxford University Press)

SUPPLEMENTARY LIST

ailiff's Daughter of Islington, The	100 Songs of England, Granville Bantock. (Oliver Ditson, Boston)
Bold Pedlar and Robin Hood, The	English Traditional Songs and Carols. L. E. Broadwood. (Boosey and Co. Ltd. London and New York)
Farmer's Son So Sweet, A	Songs of Somerset. Cecil Sharp. (Simpkin and Co. London)
Quest, The	Songs of Bohemia. Rev. Vincent Pisek. (Jan Hus Presbyterian Church, N. Y. City)
Robin Hood and the Bishop of Hereford	Folk Songs from Dorset. H. E. D. Hammond. (H. W. Gray, N.Y., N.Y.)
Spanish Lady's Love, The	Songs from Many Lands. A. Swan. (Enoch and Sons, London)
Il était une Bergère Au Clair de la Lune Sur le Pont d'Avignon	In numerous collections

Date Due